IBC対訳ライブラリー

英語で読む
オペラ座の怪人
The Phantom of the Opera

ガストン・ルルー　原著
ニーナ・ウェグナー　英文リライト
荒井惠子　英語解説
牛原眞弓　日本語訳

JN182095

カバー写真 =（左から）Alexandra Lande, Premier Photo, Bruno Passigatti / Shutterstock.com
本文写真 = Shutterstock.com
ナレーション = Howard Colefield
録音スタジオ = 株式会社巧芸創作

本書の英語テキストは、弊社から刊行されたラダーシリーズ
『The Phantom of the Opera　オペラ座の怪人』から転載しています。

『オペラ座の怪人』を楽しく読むために
——読んで、観て、聴いてください

　『オペラ座の怪人（原題は *Le Fantôme de l'Opéra*）』はフランスの作家ガストン・ルルー（Gaston Leroux）が1909年に発表した作品です。この小説をもとに、ミュージカル、映画、テレビドラマが製作され、どれも大成功を収めています。皆さんの中には、映画やミュージカルでご覧になった方も多いでしょう。本書は、その原作をシンプルな英語に書き改めたものです。英語学習者がストレスなく読み進められるよう日本語訳、語注、文法解説がついています。

　さて、英語のタイトル "*The Phantom of the Opera*" の the Opera とはパリにあるオペラ座（l'Opéra）のことで、正式名称はガルニエ宮（Palais Garnier）です。フランス人建築家のシャルル・ガルニエが設計し、13年という歳月をかけ、1875年に完成しました。当時としては最新の建築技術を用いたことで、巨大な空間を持つ絢爛豪華な歌劇場が誕生したのです。大きすぎて劇場関係者すら建物の構造をすべて把握できていなかったという話もあるほどです。それで、当時から怪人伝説がささやかれたのでしょう。物語では地下の湖が重要なシーンとなっていますが、実際のオペラ座も下水道の上に建てられたそうです。また、地下水が流れ込んで水没した地下室もあり、ガストン・ルルーが小説の舞台にオペラ座を選んだのもうなずけます。

　主人公は、新人のオペラ歌手クリスティーヌと彼女に歌の稽古をつける謎の怪人。タイトルは原題に忠実に the Phantom となっていますが、本文で「怪人」は the ghost と呼ばれています。オペラ座の複雑な構造を知り尽くし、パリの巨大な地下空間に潜む謎の怪人と、身寄りのない美しい歌手。二人を中心に、華麗なオペラ座で展開する数々のミステリアスな事件は、その真相を知る the Persian（ペルシャ人）と呼ばれる男が作者ルルーに語った話、として語られます。

物語を楽しむポイントのひとつめは、コントラスト。美しさと醜さ、優しさと残酷さ、愛と憎しみ、喜びと悲しみが、ちょうど舞台の照明と奈落の闇のように、強烈なコントラストをもって描かれ、地下の世界が象徴する孤独を際立たせています。このコントラストは、ミュージカルの舞台でも見事に表現されています。衣装の豪華さとともに、ライティングの美しさは必見です。

　物語を楽しむ2つめのポイントは、何と言っても音楽。オペラ座を舞台にした小説だけあって、オペラの舞台と音楽が、物語の背後に浮かんでくるように、効果的にオペラ作品がちりばめてあります。第3章に名前だけ出てくる『ラホールの王（*Roi de Lahore*）』は19世紀末にマスネ（Jules Massenet）によって書かれたオペラですし、主人公のクリスティーヌが出演するオペラ作品『ファウスト（*Faust*）』もグノー（Charles Gounod）が19世紀に作曲したものです。また、怪人が作曲した『勝ち誇るドンファン（*Don Juan Triumphant*）』は架空のオペラ曲ですが、モーツァルトの『ドン・ジョバンニ（*Don Giovanni*）』のイメージと重なります。物語の中に巧妙に織り込まれた、これらのオペラ作品が暗示するものを、探りながら読み進めるのも、楽しみのひとつとなるでしょう。

　ミュージカル・ファンにも嬉しい小説です。1986年にロンドンで開幕したミュージカル『オペラ座の怪人（*The Phantom of the Opera*）』は、その後もロングランを続け、海を渡ったニューヨークのブロードウェイでは最長記録を達成したそうです。日本でも劇団四季がこのミュージカルの上演を続けています。

　ではそろそろ開演です。オペラ座へようこそ。この本が皆さんをミュージカルやオペラへと誘う扉となりますように。ただし、頭上のシャンデリアには気をつけて。

荒井惠子

翻訳にあたって

　『オペラ座の怪人』は100年以上前に発表された作品ですが、今日でも多くの人に愛されている名作です。それはおそらく、奇抜な設定はもちろんのこと、そこに描かれる愛憎のうちに現代人の心に響くものがあるからでしょう。オペラ座の地下に隠れ住む「怪人」エリックは、若くて美しいクリスティーヌに恋をします。その愛は狂気じみて残酷でさえありますが、悲しいほどに一途です。異形の姿ゆえに母親からも疎んじられ、愛に飢えたエリックの渇きを、クリスティーヌは無意識ながらも感じとっていました。優柔不断にも見える彼女の態度は、女がもつ母性の表れかもしれません。

　この物語は映画やミュージカルを通して、さまざまに解釈されてきました。エリックの猟奇性を強調したものや、ラウルとの三角関係をテーマとしたものなどがあり、それぞれに見事な作品となっています。でも、わたしがいちばん胸を打たれたのは、エリックがペルシャ人にすべてを打ち明ける最後の場面でした。クリスティーヌによって心の渇きを癒されたエリックは、涙ながらにそのようすを語り、心穏やかに自分の死を受け入れます。クリスティーヌが身分違いの恋人と結婚できたのも、エリックの犠牲によるものだと思うと、本当に深い愛をもっていたのは誰だったのかと考えさせられます。

　対訳にあたっては、英語学習に用いやすくするため、できるだけ英文に忠実に訳しました。ただ、日本語として不自然なところは少し工夫し、訳文だけを読んでも楽しんでいただけるよう心がけたつもりです。ガストン・ルルーが描いた怪しくも悲しい愛の世界を、どうぞご堪能ください。

　　　　　　　　　　　　　　　　　　　　　　　　　　牛原眞弓

もくじ

PART 1

Prologue 12
序章

1. Is It the Ghost? 16
   あれは怪人？

2. The New Margarita 26
   新しいマルガリータ

3. The Rule Book 36
   職務規定書

● 覚えておきたい英語表現 46

PART 2

4. Box Five 50
   5番ボックス席

5. In Perros 60
   ペロスにて

6. *Faust* and What Followed 72
   『ファウスト』とその後

● 覚えておきたい英語表現 80

PART 3

7. The Masked Ball 86
   仮面舞踏会

8. Above the Trap-Doors...96
   隠し戸の上で

9. Erik...100
   エリック

● 覚えておきたい英語表現 116

PART 4

10. Christine! Christine!...122
    クリスティーヌ！ クリスティーヌ！

11. Down into the Cellars 130
    地下室へ

12. Inside the Torture Room...138
    拷問部屋の中

13. The Scorpion and the Grasshopper...............................156
    サソリとバッタ

● 覚えておきたい英語表現 164

PART 5

14. The End of the Ghost's Love 170
    怪人の恋の終わり

本書の構成

本書は、

- □ 英日対訳による本文
- □ 覚えておきたい英語表現
- □ 欄外の語注
- □ MP3形式の英文音声

で構成されています。

　本書は、フランスの作家ガストン・ルルー原作の『オペラ座の怪人』をやさしい英語で書きあらためた本文に、日本語訳をつけました。

　各ページの下部には、英語を読み進める上で助けとなるよう単語・熟語の意味が掲載されています。また英日の段落のはじまりが対応していますので、日本語を読んで英語を確認するという読み方もスムーズにできるようになっています。またストーリーの途中に英語解説がありますので、本文を楽しみながら、英語の使い方などをチェックしていただくのに最適です。

付属のCD-ROMについて

本書に付属のCD-ROMに収録されている音声は、パソコンや携帯音楽プレーヤーなどで再生することができるMP3ファイル形式です。一般的な音楽CDプレーヤーでは再生できませんので、ご注意ください。

■音声ファイルについて

　付属のCD-ROMには、本書の英語パートの朗読音声が収録されています。本文左ページに出てくるヘッドホンマーク内の数字とファイル名の数字がそれぞれ対応しています。

　パソコンや携帯プレーヤーで、お好きな箇所を繰り返し聴いていただくことで、発音のチェックだけでなく、英語で物語を理解する力が自然に身に付きます。

■音声ファイルの利用方法について

　CD-ROMをパソコンのCD/DVDドライブに入れて、iTunesなどの音楽再生（管理）ソフトにCD-ROM上の音声ファイルを取り込んでご利用ください。

■パソコンの音楽再生ソフトへの取り込みについて

　パソコンにMP3形式の音声ファイルを再生できるアプリケーションがインストールされていることをご確認ください。

　CD-ROMをパソコンのCD/DVDドライブに入れても、多くの場合音楽再生ソフトは自動的に起動しません。ご自分でアプリケーションを直接起動して、「ファイル」メニューから「ライブラリに追加」したり、再生ソフトのウインドウ上にファイルをマウスでドラッグ＆ドロップするなどして取り込んでください。

　音楽再生ソフトの詳しい操作方法や、携帯音楽プレーヤーへのファイルの転送方法については、ソフトやプレーヤーに付属のマニュアルで確認するか、アプリケーションの開発元にお問い合わせください。

The Phantom of the Opera

Part 1

Prologue

The opera ghost really existed. He was not just a story created by the actors, singers, and managers, or something imagined by the little dancers. He physically existed in flesh and blood, although he appeared to people as a ghost.

The story I have to tell deals with one of the saddest and most unbelievable events ever to take place at the Paris Opera House. It happened only about thirty years ago. In fact, if you visit the opera today, try asking some of the oldest men there about it. They will surely remember that event and tell you what they know.

That sad event, of course, is the kidnapping of Christine Daae, the sudden disappearance of Viscount Raoul de Chagny, and the death of his older brother, Count Philippe de Chagny, whose body was found on the shore of the underground lake that exists under the opera house.

■flesh and blood 生身の人間　■deal with ～を扱う　■Paris Opera House パリ・オペラ座　■viscount 名子爵　■count 名伯爵

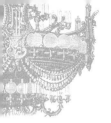

序章

　オペラ座の怪人は実在した。俳優や歌手や支配人たちの作り話でも、幼い踊り子たちの想像の産物でもなかった。人々には幽霊のように見えても、文字どおり血と肉を持って存在していたのだ。

　私がこれから語るのは、パリ・オペラ座で起こった、史上もっとも悲しく信じがたい事件の話である。起こったのは、ほんの30年前。なんなら今日オペラ座へ行って、古参の人たちに聞いてみるといい。きっと事件のことを覚えていて、知っていることを話してくれるだろう。

　その悲しい事件とはもちろん、クリスティーヌ・ダーエの誘拐、ラウル・ド・シャニー子爵の失踪、そして兄フィリップ・ド・シャニー伯爵の死である。フィリップの亡骸は、オペラ座の下にある地下湖の畔で発見された。

When I began studying this terrible story at the National Academy of Music, I was surprised by how many connections there seemed to be between the "ghost" and the disappearance of these three people. Nobody who was there at the time seemed to think the ghost had anything to do with the disappearance of Christine Daae. But I slowly began to think that somehow the ghost was responsible for the terrible event.

I discovered that my beliefs were correct when I talked with the man known throughout Paris simply as "the Persian." The man had been there and witnessed some parts of the event. Greatly excited, I listened to his story. When he finished, he handed me evidence that the ghost existed, including the strange letters of Christine Daae. Finally I could not doubt the story anymore. The ghost was real!

■National Academy of Music 国立音楽アカデミー《パリ・オペラ座のこと》 ■at the time その当時 ■responsible for 〜の原因である ■witness 動 〜を目撃する

この国立音楽アカデミーでの悲惨な物語について調べ始めた時、「怪人」と3人の失踪の間に深い関係があるらしいと気づいて、私は驚いた。当時は、クリスティーヌ・ダーエの失踪に怪人が関わっていると思う者は誰もいなかった。だが私は次第に、怪人がなんらかの形で、この悲惨な事件を引き起こしたのではないかと考えるようになった。

　自分の考えが正しいとわかったのは、パリじゅうでただ「ペルシャ人」としてのみ知られている男と話した時だった。その男は現場にいて、事件の一部を目撃したのだ。私は胸を躍らせながら、彼の話を聞いた。ペルシャ人は話し終えると、怪人が存在した証拠を差しだした。そこには、クリスティーヌ・ダーエの奇妙な手紙も含まれていた。もはや疑う余地はない。怪人は本当にいたのだ！

1. Is It the Ghost?

We'll begin our story on the evening that Mr. Debienne and Mr. Poligny, the managers of the opera, were throwing their retirement party. La Sorelli, one of the main dancers, was in her dressing room going over the speech she was to give for the two retiring managers. Suddenly, her door opened and a group of young dancers rushed into the room.

"It's the ghost!" cried little Jammes, one of the ballet girls. She locked the door.

Sorelli believed in ghosts. Little Jammes's words made her hands shake, but she tried to look calm.

"Have you seen him?" asked Sorelli.

"Yes! As plainly as I see you now!" said Jammes.

"He is very ugly!" added another dancer.

The dancers described what they had seen: a gentleman in dress clothes who suddenly appeared before them in the hall. He seemed to have come straight through a wall.

■throw a party パーティーをひらく ■dressing room 楽屋 ■go over 〜を練習する ■be to do 〜する予定である ■believe in 〜を信じる ■plainly 副 はっきりと

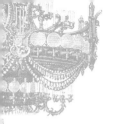

1. あれは怪人？

 それではまず、オペラ座の支配人、ドビエンヌ氏とポリニー氏が引退記念パーティーを開いた夜から話を始めよう。主役をつとめるバレリーナの1人、ラ・ソレリは楽屋で、引退する2人の支配人に送るためのスピーチの練習をしていた。するといきなりドアが開き、若い踊り子たちがひとかたまりになって部屋に飛び込んできた。

 「怪人よ！」バレエの踊り子の1人、少女のジャムが叫んだ。そしてドアに鍵をかけた。
 ソレリは怪人の存在を信じていた。小さなジャムの言葉に手が震えたが、平静を装った。
 「怪人を見たの？」と、ソレリは聞いた。
 「はい！ 今あなたを見てるみたいに、はっきりと！」とジャム。
 「とっても醜かったわ！」と、他の踊り子が付け加えた。
 踊り子たちは今見たものを説明してみせた——正装した紳士が、廊下で目の前に突然現れたのだ。壁をすっと通り抜けてきたようだという。

For several months now, all anybody at the opera had talked about was this ghost in dress clothes who appeared in different parts of the building. He spoke to nobody and disappeared as soon as he was seen. He made no noise when walking.

At first people laughed at the stories, but the ghost's fame grew and grew. Finally, any accident or strange event was blamed on the ghost. Every fall, every broken object, and every ballet shoe that went missing was thought to be the work of the opera ghost.

The girls all said the ghost was a skeleton with a death's head. This description had actually come from Joseph Buquet, the head scene-changer. He had *really* seen the ghost, unlike many of the ballet girls who often talked about the ghost but hadn't actually seen him. Joseph had seen him on a narrow, dark staircase that led down to the cellars of the opera.

"He is terribly thin, and his clothes hang on him as if on a skeleton," Joseph said. "His eyes are so deep they look like two black holes, just like in a dead man's skull. He has no nose. He has no hair either, except for three long, dark locks behind his ears!"

■dress clothes 正装 ■blame on（罪などを）〜のせいにする ■staircase 图階段
■as if まるで〜であるかのように ■lock 图髪の毛の房

ここ数か月、オペラ座じゅうの人がいつも話題にしているのは、建物のさまざまな場所に現れるこの正装した怪人のことだった。怪人は誰にも話しかけず、見つかるとすぐに姿を消した。そして音を立てずに歩いた。

　初めのうち人々はその話を笑いとばしていたが、怪人の噂はますます広がっていった。そしてとうとう、事故や変わった事件があると、なんでも怪人のせいにされるようになった。何かが落ちたのも、壊れたのも、バレエシューズがなくなったのも、すべてオペラ座の怪人の仕業だと思われた。

　少女たちはみんな、怪人はどくろの顔をした骸骨だと言った。じつはこの表現は道具方主任のジョゼフ・ビュケが言いだしたものだ。怪人の噂ばかりしながら実際には見たことがない踊り子たちと違って、ジョゼフは本当に怪人を目にしたことがあった。オペラ座の地下室へ通じる、狭くて暗い階段で怪人を目撃したのだ。

　「ひどくやせててさ、骸骨に服を引っかけてるみたいなんだ」と、ジョゼフは言った。「目はひどく落ち込んでて、2つの黒い穴みたいに見える。あれじゃまるで、どくろだな。それに鼻がない。髪の毛もほとんどなくて、耳の後ろに長くて黒い髪が3房あるだけさ！」

But let us return to the evening we were discussing.

"Listen!" said little Jammes as she put her ear to the door. Everyone fell silent, and they all listened hard. There was a slight sound outside—was it the sound of footsteps? Then it stopped, and there was only silence.

Sorelli, trying to look calm, went to the door and called out, "Who's there?"

There was no reply.

Sorelli suddenly opened the door and cried out, "Who's there?"

There was only an empty, dark hall. She quickly shut the door and turned to the girls.

"Nobody's there," she said. Then, secretly, so no one would see, she made the sign of the cross with her right hand.

"But we saw him!" said Jammes. "And yesterday, Gabriel the song-master saw him too! Gabriel was so afraid that he jumped up from his chair and hit his head on a hat peg. Then, hurrying out of the room he tripped and fell down the stairs! It was all the ghost's doing, you see!"

Then little Giry spoke up.

"My mother says we shouldn't talk about such things," she said.

■listen hard 耳をすます ■call out 呼びかける ■cry out 叫ぶ ■make a sign of the cross 手で十字架の形に空を切る ■peg 図(物をかけるための)くぎ ■trip 動つまずく ■you see ご存知の通り，ほらね ■speak up はっきりと言う

しかしこのあたりで、先ほど話していた夜に話を戻そう。
「ねえ、聞いて！」と、小さなジャムがドアに耳を押し当てて言った。皆が静まりかえって、聞き耳を立てた。外でかすかな音がする——足音だろうか？　ふと音がやんで、静寂だけが残った。

　ソレリは落ち着いたふりをしながら、ドアに近づいて声をかけた。「どなた？」
　答えはなかった。
　ソレリはいきなりドアを開け、大声をあげた。「誰なの？」

　からっぽの暗い廊下があるだけだ。ソレリはすばやくドアを閉め、少女たちに向き直った。
「誰もいないわ」と言った。そして誰にも気づかれないよう、こっそりと右手で十字を切った。
「でも、見たんだもの！」とジャム。「それに昨日、声楽主任のガブリエルさんも見たのよ！　あの人、すごく怖かったから、椅子から跳び上がって帽子掛けに頭をぶつけたのよ。そしてあわてて部屋を出て、つまずいて階段から落ちちゃったの！　全部怪人の仕業よ、そうでしょ！」

　すると、少女のジリーがはっきりした声で言った。
「そんなこと話しちゃいけないって、母さんが言ってるわ」

"Why not?" said the girls, crowding around her. "Why not?"

"I—I promised I wouldn't tell!"

But the girls kept crowding around her and promised to keep her secret, so little Giry told them all that she knew.

"The ghost has a private box!"

"A box! At the opera? Tell us more!" said the ballet girls.

"Yes, it's Box Five. You know, on the top level, next to the stage-box. My mother is in charge of it. And she says nobody has used that box for a whole month except the ghost. The managers' office has ordered that tickets to that box must never be sold."

The girls stared with wide eyes.

"The ghost comes to the box and my mother gives him his program, but she has never seen him. The truth is he can't be seen! Do you understand? He has no dress clothes or a death's head! So all this talk about a skeleton isn't true! And my mother says talking about it will bring us bad luck."

Just then, they heard heavy footsteps in the hall, and someone called out, "Cecile Jammes! Are you there?"

■box 図ボックス席《一般席から隔てられた特別席》　■stage-box 図舞台脇の特別席
■in charge of ～を担当して　■bad luck 災難

「どうして？」と少女たちが言って、ジリーを取り囲んだ。「どうしていけないの？」

「あ、あたし——言わないって約束したもの！」

でも、少女たちはジリーを取り囲んだまま離そうとせず、秘密を守るからと約束したので、小さなジリーは知っていることをすべて話してしまった。

「怪人は専用のボックス席を持ってるのよ！」

「ボックス席ですって？　オペラ座に？　もっと話して！」と、踊り子の少女たち。

「ほんとよ、5番ボックス席。ほら、最上級の、舞台横のボックス席の隣よ。母さんが担当してるの。もうまる1か月も、怪人以外にあのボックス席を使った人はいないんだって。支配人室から、あのボックス席の切符は売らないようにって言われてるのよ」

少女たちは目をみはってジリーを見つめた。

「怪人がボックス席に来たら、母さんがプログラムを渡すんだけど、姿を見たことがないの。というより、見えないのよ！　わかる？　正装もどくろもないの！　だから骸骨だとかいう話はうそよ！　それに母さんは、このことを話したらよくないことがあるって言ってるわ」

ちょうどそのとき、廊下に重々しい足音がして、誰かが大声で呼んだ。「セシル・ジャム！　そこにいるの？」

"It's mother!" said little Jammes. She opened the door, and a rather large woman rushed into the room and dropped herself onto the sofa.

"It's so terrible!" she cried out.

"What, mother? What's happened?"

"Joseph Buquet is dead! He was found hanging in the third-floor cellar!"

The girls cried out and they all started talking at once.

"It's the ghost!" someone said.

"I shall never be able to give my speech," said Sorelli, closing her eyes.

The truth is, no one ever knew how Joseph Buquet died. The examiner said Joseph had killed himself. However, there are details that remain a mystery. When the managers were notified of the death, they had workers go to the cellar to cut the body down. But when they arrived, the body had already been cut down and the rope had disappeared.

■drop oneself onto ～の上に倒れこむ　■cellar 名 地下室　■shall never 決して～ない　■examiner 名 検査官　■detail 名 細部

「母さんだわ！」と小さなジャム。彼女がドアを開けると、かなり大柄な女が部屋にあわてて入ってきて、ソファーに座りこんだ。

「ああ、ほんとに恐ろしいわ！」と、女が叫んだ。
「なんなの、母さん？　何があったの？」
「ジョゼフ・ビュケが亡くなったのよ！　地下３階の部屋で首をつっているのが見つかったの！」
少女たちは叫び声をあげ、いっせいに話しはじめた。
「怪人がやったのよ！」と、誰かが言った。
「スピーチなんて、とてもできそうにないわ」と、ソレリが目を閉じて言った。
　じつは、ジョゼフ・ビュケがどのように死んだのか誰にもわからなかった。検死官によれば、ジョゼフは自殺したのだという。それでも、いくつかの点が謎のままだ。支配人たちはその死の知らせを受けて、従業員を地下室へ行かせ、ロープを切って死体を降ろすように命じた。ところが地下室に着くと、死体はすでに降ろされて、ロープがなくなっていたのだ。

2. The New Margarita

That same evening, Count Philippe de Chagny had brought his younger brother, Raoul, to his private box at the opera. Raoul was a young sailor and he had just returned to Paris several weeks ago after sailing around the world. He was a rather shy young man, and he had very soft, pretty features. Count Philippe was twenty years older than Raoul and was very proud of him.

Ever since his return, Raoul had taken up a great love for the opera. Also, Philippe was rather close with La Sorelli, and he thought Raoul might like to be introduced to some of the other beauties of the opera.

■feature 图顔だち ■be proud of ～を誇りに思う ■take up （趣味などを）始める
■be close with ～と近しい仲である

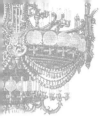

2. 新しいマルガリータ

　その同じ夜、フィリップ・ド・シャニー伯爵が、弟のラウルをオペラ座の自分のボックス席へ連れてきていた。ラウルは若い航海士で、世界中を航海した後、数週間前にパリへ戻ってきたところだった。いくぶん内気な若者で、じつに穏やかな美しい顔立ちをしている。フィリップ伯爵はラウルより20歳年上で、弟のことをとても自慢に思っていた。

　パリに戻ってからというもの、ラウルはすっかりオペラ座に夢中だった。それにフィリップはラ・ソレリといい仲だったので、ラウルにもオペラ座の他の美女たちを紹介してやれば喜ぶだろうと思ったのだ。

That evening, Christine Daae had shocked everyone with her version of *Faust*. She was a good singer, but she was never *great*, so Christine had been given only the smaller parts in the opera. However, that night, La Carlotta, the opera's main star, had fallen ill. Someone had to take the part of Margarita, one of the most important parts in *Faust*. In a rush, the managers told Christine to do it. They hadn't expected much. So, you can imagine everybody's surprise when she made her entrance and sang like an angel. No one had ever heard anything like it. That night, Christine showed Paris a new kind of Margarita—a splendid, haunting Margarita.

Everyone was shocked. Had Christine been hiding her true voice all this time? If so, why? Had the managers known that Christine had such a voice? Is that why they had chosen her, who had never been very good, to take the role of Margarita at the last minute? It was odd, because it was well-known that Christine did not have a professor of music at the time. She often said that she wanted to practice alone. It was all a mystery.

At the end of her song, as everyone jumped up and cheered for Christine, she fainted on stage.

■Faust 名『ファウスト』《ゲーテの劇詩を題材にしたオペラ》 ■take the part of ～の役を演じる ■make one's entrance 登場する ■splendid 形光り輝く ■haunting 形記憶に長く残る ■at the last minute 直前になって ■faint 動気絶する

その夜、クリスティーヌ・ダーエは彼女なりの『ファウスト』を演じて、皆を驚かせた。彼女はいい歌手だったが、素晴らしいというほどでもなかったので、オペラ座ではずっと端役だった。しかしこの夜、主役歌手のラ・カルロッタが病気になったのだ。『ファウスト』のもっとも重要な役のひとつであるマルガリータを、誰かが演じなければならない。慌てた支配人たちはクリスティーヌにそれを命じたが、大して期待してはいなかった。だから、彼女が舞台に上がり、天使のように歌った時の皆の驚きようは想像できるだろう。これまで誰も、そのような歌を聞いたことがなかった。その夜、クリスティーヌは新しいタイプのマルガリータ——燦然と輝く、忘れがたいマルガリータをパリの人々に見せつけたのだ。

　皆が衝撃を受けた。クリスティーヌはこれまで本当の声を隠していたのだろうか？　もしそうなら、なぜそんなことを？　支配人たちは、クリスティーヌがこのような声をしていると知っていたのか？　だから、これまで大したことのなかった彼女を、直前になってマルガリータの役に選んだのか？　だが、それはおかしい。というのも、当時クリスティーヌが音楽の教師についていなかったことは、よく知られていたからだ。彼女は１人で練習したいといつも言っていた。すべては謎だった。

　歌が終わり、観客全員が立ち上がってクリスティーヌに歓声を送っていると、彼女は舞台で気を失って倒れてしまった。

Philippe turned to his brother and saw Raoul was quite pale.

"She just fainted!" Raoul said. He looked like he was going to faint himself. "Let's go see her. She never sang like that before."

Before Philippe could stop him, Raoul was headed to the *foyer de ballet*, walking past all the ballet girls, and turning into the hall that led to the dressing room of Christine Daae. Philippe thought it was strange that Raoul knew the way.

A crowd of people had gathered around Christine's room. They had all been excited by Christine's performance, as well as her fainting fit. The doctor arrived at the same time as Raoul. Christine was lying unconscious on the sofa.

"Doctor," said Raoul with a concerned face, "shouldn't you clear all these people out of here?"

The doctor agreed, and everyone was told to leave the room except for Christine, her maid, Raoul, and the doctor. Raoul simply acted like he should be there and the doctor did not kick him out.

When Christine finally awoke, Raoul was right next to her.

■pale 形青ざめた　■head to ～へ向かう　■foyer de ballet バレリーナ共同控え室　■walk past 通り過ぎる　■as well as ～と同様に　■fit 名発作　■clear 動～を立ち退かせる　■kick someone out （人を）追い出す　■right next to ～のすぐ隣に

フィリップが弟のほうを向くと、ラウルは真っ青になっていた。

「気を失ったぞ！」ラウルが言った。まるで自分が失神しそうだった。「様子を見に行こう。これまであんなふうに歌ったことはなかったんだ」

フィリップが止める間もなく、ラウルはバレエの稽古場へ向かい、踊り子の少女たち皆の脇をすり抜けて、クリスティーヌ・ダーエの楽屋へ通じる廊下へ曲がっていった。フィリップは、なぜラウルが行き方を知っているのだろうと不思議に思った。

クリスティーヌの部屋のあたりには、人が群がっていた。クリスティーヌの演技にも、また失神したことにも、みんな興奮していた。医者がラウルと同時に到着した。クリスティーヌは意識のないままソファーに寝かされている。

「先生」と、ラウルは心配そうな顔で言った。「この人たちをみんな外へ出した方がいいんじゃないですか？」

医者はそれに賛成した。クリスティーヌとメイド、ラウル、医者以外は全員部屋から出るよう命じられた。いかにもそこにいるべき人間のようにふるまったラウルは、追い出されずにすんだ。

クリスティーヌがやっと目を覚ました時、ラウルは彼女のすぐそばにいた。

"Excuse me, sir," she said in a whisper, "but who are you?"

At this, Raoul got on his knee, kissed her hand, and said, "I am the little boy who went into the sea to save your scarf!"

This was such a strange thing to say that Christine began to laugh and was joined by the doctor and her maid. Raoul turned red.

"Miss Daae," he said, "if you do not recognize me, then I would like to say something to you in private—something important."

"Perhaps later," said Christine, sitting up. "Please, all of you, leave me. I need some peace."

Everyone, including the doctor, left the room. After Christine's door closed, Raoul stayed in the hall, waiting for her to come out so he might speak to her. But he soon heard voices come from inside her room!

"Christine, you must love me!" said a man's voice. It sounded clear, strong, and rather demanding.

"How can you say that?" said Christine. "I sing only for you!"

She sounded as though she were crying.

"Are you tired?" asked the voice, more gently now.

■get on one's knee ひざまずく　■save 動 ～を救い出す　■sit up（寝た姿勢から）上体を起こす　■demanding 形 催促がましい　■as though まるで～するかのように

「あの、すみません」彼女はささやいた。「どなたですか？」
　すると、ラウルは片ひざをついて彼女の手にキスをし、こう言った。「あなたのスカーフを取りに海へ入った少年ですよ！」
　あまりにも唐突な答えだったので、クリスティーヌは笑いだし、医者とメイドも一緒に笑った。ラウルの顔が赤くなった。

「ダーエさん」とラウル。「私がおわかりにならないのなら、２人だけで話をさせてください——とても大切なことです」

「後にしていただけますか」とクリスティーヌは言って、体を起こした。「どうか皆さん、私を１人にしてください。少し静かにしていたいんです」
　医者も含めて、皆が部屋を出た。クリスティーヌの部屋のドアが閉まった後、ラウルは廊下に残り、彼女が出てきたら話しかけようと待っていた。ところが、しばらくすると部屋の中から声が聞こえてきたのだ！

「クリスティーヌ、君は私を愛さねばならない！」と、男の声がした。はっきりとした、力強い、そしてかなり強引な声だった。
「どうしてそんなことを言うの？」とクリスティーヌ。「あなたのためだけに歌っているのに！」
　彼女は泣いているようだった。
「疲れたかい？」と、声が今度はもっとやさしく尋ねた。

"Tired? Tonight I gave you my soul and now I am dead!" she said.

"Your soul is beautiful," said the man, "and I thank you. No king ever received so wonderful a gift. Tonight you made the angels weep."

Raoul heard nothing after that. He was filled with love for one person in that room and hatred for the other. As his anger grew stronger, he suddenly heard the door open. He rushed to hide in the shadow of the hall, and he saw Christine, alone, pass him. When she disappeared down the hall, Raoul jumped into Christine's room, ready to meet the man with the clear, strong voice.

"Who's there?" he cried out.

There was no sound. Raoul turned on the lamps. He searched everywhere—but there was no one in the room.

■no A ever かつてどんなAも〜ない　■make someone do（人に）〜させる　■weep 動 泣く　■pass 動 〜を通り過ぎる　■jump into 〜に飛び込む　■turn on（照明などを）つける

「疲れたかですって？　今夜あなたに魂を捧げたから、今は死んでいるのも同じよ！」

「君の魂は美しい」と男。「ありがとう。たとえ王であろうと、こんなに素晴らしい贈り物をもらった者はいないよ。今夜の君には天使さえ泣いただろう。」

その後ラウルには何も聞こえなかった。彼は、その部屋にいる1人への愛にあふれ、もう1人への憎しみに満ちていた。怒りがさらに強くなった時、突然ドアの開く音がした。ラウルは慌てて廊下の陰に隠れ、クリスティーヌが1人で通り過ぎていくのを見た。彼女が廊下の奥に消えた時、ラウルは部屋に飛び込み、あのはっきりとした力強い声の男と対面しようとした。

「そこにいるのは誰だ？」ラウルは大声をあげた。

だが、なんの音もしない。ラウルはランプをつけた。あらゆるところを探した——しかし部屋には誰もいなかった。

3. The Rule Book

During this time, the retiring managers, Mr. Debienne and Mr. Poligny, were talking and laughing with their party guests. Sorelli and the dancers had made it to the *foyer de ballet* where Sorelli was about to make her speech. Nobody at the party yet knew about Joseph Buquet's death except for the ballet girls.

However, just as Sorelli had put on her famous smile, lifted her wine glass, and started to speak, her speech was cut short by little Jammes.

"The opera ghost!" cried out Jammes. She pointed toward the back of the crowd. But by the time the guests turned around to see who was there, the ghost had slipped away. He was gone.

The guests started laughing, believing it was a joke.

"The opera ghost!" they said as they pointed to their friends.

■make it to 〜に到着する ■except for 〜を除いて ■just as 〜の途端に ■put on a smile 笑顔を作る ■cut short 〜を途中で止める ■slip away こっそり立ち去る

3. 職務規定書

　その頃、引退する支配人のドビエンヌ氏とポリニー氏は、パーティーの招待客と歓談していた。ソレリと踊り子たちがバレエの稽古場へやってきた。ソレリはここでスピーチすることになっていたのだ。パーティーでジョゼフ・ビュケの死を知っている者は、踊り子の少女たち以外に誰もいなかった。

　ところが、ちょうどソレリが評判の美しい笑顔を浮かべ、ワイングラスを掲げて話しはじめた時、小さなジャムの声がスピーチを遮った。

　「オペラ座の怪人よ！」とジャムは叫んだ。そして人混みの後ろを指さした。だが客たちが振り返って確かめる前に、怪人はするりと逃げ、消え去ってしまった。

　客たちは、てっきり冗談だと思って笑い出した。
　「オペラ座の怪人だ！」客たちは友人たちを指して言いあった。

Sorelli, of course, was angry. She did not get to finish her speech, but the retiring managers thanked her and kissed her, then hurried up the stairs to the *foyer* of the singers. The singers and musicians were gathered there to make a speech for the managers also. After this was done, finally, on the third floor, the managers met their own guests and friends, who were gathered to make their speeches and to have dinner together.

It was here, on the third floor, that the old managers met the new managers, Mr. Moncharmin and Mr. Richard. They greeted the men who were to take over the opera the next day. The crowd around them settled into talk and laughter. It was during these pleasant moments when a few people began to notice a very thin, very ugly man sitting at the dinner table by himself.

The man had deep-set eyes, so deep that they looked like two black holes in his head. His dress clothes hung on him as though he were a skeleton. He was terrible to look at, but most people simply turned away and politely said nothing. So it was the opera ghost himself who spoke first.

■hurry up stairs 急いで階段を上がる ■take over（仕事などを）引き継ぐ ■settle into ～に腰を据える ■deep-set 深くくぼんだ ■turn away（顔などを）背ける

ソレリはもちろん怒っていた。最後までスピーチできなかったが、引退する支配人たちはソレリに感謝してキスをし、それから急いで階段を上って歌手の稽古場へ向かった。そこでも歌手と音楽家たちが、支配人たちに送辞を述べようと集まっているからだ。これが終わると、ようやく支配人たちは３階で自分の客や友人たちと顔を合わせた。この人たちも、送辞と会食のために集まっていた。

　この３階で前支配人たちは、新しい支配人のモンシャルマン氏とリシャール氏に会った。そして、翌日からオペラ座を引き継ぐ両氏と挨拶を交わした。まわりの人たちは歓談を始めた。この楽しいひとときの間のことだった。ひどくやせて、ひじょうに醜い男がたったひとりで夕食の席に着いていることに、数人の客が気づきだしたのだ。

　男の目はくぼんでいたが、それがあまりに深いので、顔に２つの黒い穴が開いているようだった。正装の服は、骸骨に着せたように垂れ下がっている。おぞましい外見だったが、ほとんどの人はただ目をそらし、礼儀をわきまえて何も言わなかった。だから真っ先に口を開いたのは、オペラ座の怪人自身だった。

"The death of Joseph Buquet is perhaps not a natural death," he said.

All talk in the room stopped.

"Is Buquet dead?" the old managers cried out.

"Yes," said the ghost. "He was found hanging in the third-floor cellar, between a set piece and a scene from the *Roi de Lahore*."

The managers turned white. They asked the new managers to join them in the manager's office. Once they had closed the door behind them, they asked the two new managers to sit, for they had a secret to tell them.

"Do you know who that man sitting at the table is?" Mr. Poligny asked Mr. Moncharmin and Mr. Richard. The new managers said no.

"That is the opera ghost," said Mr. Poligny. "He has ordered us to ask you, as the new managers, to give him anything he wants."

The new managers looked at each other and began laughing.

"What kind of joke is this?" asked Mr. Richard. But the old managers just stared at him, their faces like stone.

■set piece（舞台の）大道具　■scene（劇などの）書き割り、背景　■Roi de Lahore『ラホールの王』《ジュール・マスネ作曲のオペラ》　■turn white　真っ青になる

「ジョゼフ・ビュケの死は、どうも普通の死ではないようだな」と言った。

部屋じゅうの話し声がぴたりと止んだ。
「ビュケが死んだって？」前支配人たちが大声をあげた。
「そうとも」と怪人。「地下３階の部屋で首をつって発見された。『ラホールの王』の大道具と書き割りの間でね」

支配人たちは真っ青になった。そして新しい支配人たちに、支配人室へ一緒に来るように頼んだ。中に入ってドアを閉めると、２人の新支配人に座るよう促した。彼らに話すべき秘密があったからだ。

「テーブルに座っていたあの男を知っていますか？」ポリニー氏は、モンシャルマン氏とリシャール氏に尋ねた。新支配人たちは、知らないと答えた。
「あれはオペラ座の怪人です」とポリニー氏。「私たちは、彼の望む物を何でも差しだすよう、新支配人のあなたたちに頼んでおくようにと命じられたのです」
新支配人たちはお互いに顔を見合わせて、笑いだした。

「これはなんの冗談ですか？」と、リシャール氏が聞いた。しかし前支配人たちはただ彼を見つめるだけで、その表情は石のように硬かった。

"This is not a joke," said Mr. Poligny. "Every time we do something that the ghost doesn't like, something terrible happens at the opera. The death of Joseph Buquet is the latest example."

"Well, what does the ghost want from us?" asked Mr. Richard. He tried to hide his smile, but he failed.

Mr. Poligny went to his desk and pulled out the rule book, which has been given to every manager since the start of the opera. The book stated that the manager of the opera would lose his job if he did not follow four rules. The rules were listed from one through four. At the end, a fifth rule had been written into the book by hand, in red ink, in very strange, child-like writing. It read:

"5. If the manager is late in paying the opera ghost the amount of twenty thousand francs a month, for a total of two hundred forty thousand francs a year, the manager shall be made to leave the opera."

"This was written by the ghost, you see?" said Mr. Debienne.

■latest 形 最新の　■pull out 取り出す　■state 動 (公式に) 明言する　■follow a rule 規則に従う　■by hand 手書きで　■franc フラン《かつてフランスで定められていた通貨》

「冗談などではありません」とポリニー氏。「私たちが怪人の気に入らないことをするたびに、オペラ座に恐ろしいことが起こるのです。ジョゼフ・ビュケの死が、もっとも最近の例ですよ」

「それじゃあ、怪人はいったい何が望みなのです？」と、リシャール氏が尋ねた。笑みを隠そうとしたが、うまくいかなかった。

ポリニー氏は自分の机に近寄り、引き出しから職務規定書を取り出した。それは、オペラ座ができた時から、すべての支配人に渡されてきたものだ。その規定書には、オペラ座の支配人は4つの規則を守らなければ職を解かれると書かれていた。規則は第1から第4まで列挙されている。そして最後に5番目の規則が、赤いインクの手書きで、しかもじつに奇妙な、子どもが書いたような字で書かれていた。内容はこうだった。

「第5．もし支配人が、月に2万フラン、つまり年に合計24万フランの金をオペラ座の怪人に支払うのが遅れたら、支配人はオペラ座を去らねばならない」

「これは怪人が書いたのです、おわかりですか？」とドビエンヌ氏。

"Is this all?" asked Mr. Richard, who still believed this was all a very fine joke. "Doesn't he want anything else?"

"Yes," replied Mr. Poligny. He turned a few pages in the rule book and came to the part that listed the days in which certain private boxes must be made free for the president, the ministers, and so on. Here, again, a line had been added in red ink:

"Box Five on the top level shall be saved for the use of the opera ghost for every performance."

At this, the two new managers looked at each other and laughed out loud again.

"Very good, sirs, very good," they said, rising from their chairs. They shook the retiring managers' hands and left the room laughing.

"I see that we French are still excellent at creating jokes!" said Mr. Moncharmin. The two enjoyed the rest of the party without another thought about the opera ghost.

■make free 空けておく　■and so on ～など　■save for ～に備えて使わないでおく
■see that ... ～ということが分かる

「これで全部ですか？」とリシャール氏は聞いたが、すべてがよくできたジョークだと、まだ思っていた。「他にも何か欲しがってるものはありませんか？」

「ありますとも」と、ポリニー氏は答えた。そして規定書のページを繰り、大統領や首相たちのために、特定のボックス席を空けておくべき日を記した箇所を開いた。ここにもまた、赤いインクの１行が書き加えられていた。

「最上級の５番ボックス席は、あらゆる公演でオペラ座の怪人専用として取っておくこと」

これを見て、２人の新支配人は顔を見合わせ、再び大声で笑った。

「素晴らしい、いやあ、じつに素晴らしい」２人はそう言って、椅子から立ち上がった。そして引退する支配人たちと握手を交わし、笑いながら部屋を出ていった。

「我々フランス人は、まだジョークを生み出すのがうまいようだな！」と、モンシャルマン氏が言った。それから２人は最後までパーティーを楽しみ、もうオペラ座の怪人のことなど思い出しもしなかった。

覚えておきたい英語表現［文法］

make/let/have + O + 動詞の原形

基本文法をおさらいすると、読みが確実になります。物語を楽しみながら、合わせて文法力もつけましょう。ここでは、使役動詞を使った「make/let/have + O + 動詞の原形」に注目します。S（主語）、V（動詞）、O（目的語）、C（補語）はほとんどの場合、決まった順番に並んでいますから、この文構造をつかむことが英文読解の正確さにつながります。

Little Jammes's words <u>made her hands shake</u>, but she tried to look calm. (p.16, 9行目)
ジャムの言葉に手が震えたが、彼女は平静を装った。

【解説】shake hands（握手する）という表現を思い浮かべた方も多いかもしれませんが、ここでshakeするのはhandsで、そうさせた（made）のはLittle Jammes's wordsです。

madeは使役動詞makeの過去形。「make + O + 動詞の原形」の形で、「Oを〜させる」となっています。文の前半を直訳すると、「ジャムの言葉が彼女の手を震わせた」、つまり「ジャムの言葉を聞いて手が震えた」という意味になります。SVOCの典型的パターンです。C（補語）の位置にあるのは、原形不定詞（動詞の原形）です。

文の主語はLittle Jammes's wordsです。日本語は生きているものが主語になりますが、英語では無生物が主語になることがよくあります。

makeは主語が人の場合は、通例「強制的に〜させる」という意味になりますが、主語が無生物の場合は、強制的なニュアンスはありません。

【例文】 What <u>made you change</u> your mind?
何があなたに気を変えさせたのですか→どうして気が変わったのですか？

These shoes will <u>make your legs look</u> long and slim.
この靴はあなたの足をすらりと長く見せるでしょう→この靴をはけば足がすらりと長く見えますよ。

> Tonight you <u>made the angels weep</u>. (p.34, 4行目)
> 今夜の君には天使さえも泣いただろう。

【解説】同じく使役動詞のmakeですが、主語が人です。you（クリスティーヌ）があまりにすばらしくて、天使ですら、こらえようとしても涙がこぼれてくる感じが出ています。

【例文】　He <u>made me promise</u> to keep quiet.
　　　　彼は私に黙っているよう約束させた→私に口止めした。

　　　　Don't <u>make me worry</u>.
　　　　私を心配させるな→心配かけないでちょうだい。

> 5. If the manager is late in paying the opera ghost the amount of twenty thousand francs a month, for a total of two hundred forty thousand francs a year, the manager shall <u>be made to leave</u> the opera. (p.42, 下から6行目)
> 第5．もし支配人が、月に2万フラン、つまり年に合計24万フランを、オペラ座の怪人に支払うのが遅れたら、支配人はオペラ座を去らねばならない。

【解説】主節の部分the manager shall be made to leave the operaに使役動詞makeの受動態が使われています。直訳すれば「支配人はオペラ座を去るように（強制）されるであろう」となり、強制するのは実際は怪人なので、I shall make the manager leave the opera.となるところですが、ルールとして書かれていますから、the managerを主語にして受動態になっています。
　「make + O + 動詞の原形」の形が受動態になると、「be made + to不定詞」となります。動詞の原形（原形不定詞）がto不定詞に変わることに注意してください。ちなみに、shallは話し手の意志を表します。ここでは特に「～することになろう」と、厳かな予告や宣告の雰囲気が出ています。

【例文】　Her students <u>were made to learn</u> 50 English words every week.
　　　　彼女の生徒たちは毎週英単語を50個覚えさせられた。

> He turned a few pages in the rule book and came to the part that listed the days in which <u>certain private boxes must be made free</u> for the president, the ministers, and so on.
> (p.44, 3行目)
>
> 彼は規定書のページを繰り、大統領や首相たちのために、特定のボックス席を空けておくべき日を記した箇所を開いた。

【解説】「make + O + 形容詞」の場合は、受動態になっても形容詞はそのままです。

【例文】　It should <u>be made clear</u> who made the decisions.
　　　　　誰が決定したのか明らかにされるべきだ。

> When the managers were notified of the death, they <u>had workers go</u> to the cellar to cut the body down. (p.24, 下から4行目)
> 支配人たちはその死の知らせを受けて、従業員を地下室へ行かせ、ロープを切って死体を降ろすように命じた。

【解説】haveもmakeと同じ文型をとって、「have + O + 動詞の原形」で、「Oに〜させる」と、使役の意味を表わしますが、makeと違って、目上の者が目下の者に「〜させる」、しかるべき職業の人に「〜してもらう」ときに使います。主節の部分の直訳は「彼らは、ロープを切って死体を降ろすために、従業員を地下室に行かせた」。

【例文】　Shall I <u>have Ms. Arai call</u> you back later?
　　　　　後ほど荒井に折り返し電話させましょうか。

　　　　　You should <u>have a repairer fix</u> this air conditioner.
　　　　　このエアコン、修理屋に直してもらった方がいいよ。

Part 2

4. Box Five

Mr. Richard and Mr. Moncharmin enjoyed the first few days of being the new managers of the opera. They were very excited about working for such a famous institution. They forgot all about what the old managers had told them about the rule book and the ghost. Then, one morning, they received a letter that proved that the joke (if it was, indeed, a joke) was not over.

The letter was written in the same red ink and child-like writing as the lines added to the rule book. The letter read:

Dear Mr. Manager,

I'm sorry to trouble you during this busy time. However, I had to bring to your attention something very important: I have found, on a few occasions, that my private box at

■institution 图（公共の）施設　■prove 動 ～ということを証明する　■be over 終わる　■bring to someone's attention （人に）気づかせる

4. 5番ボックス席

　リシャール氏とモンシャルマン氏はオペラ座の支配人として、最初の数日を機嫌よく過ごした。これほど有名な劇場で働くことに心が弾んだ。そして前支配人たちから聞いた職務規定書や怪人の話など、すっかり忘れていた。ところがある朝、1通の手紙を受け取り、例のジョークが（もし本当にジョークならだが）終わっていないことがわかったのだ。

　その手紙は、職務規定書に書き加えられたものと同じ赤いインクを使い、子どものような字で書かれていた。手紙の内容はこうだった。

　　拝啓　支配人殿

　お忙しいところをお邪魔して申し訳ない。しかしながら、たいへん重要なことを指摘しなければならなくなった。ここ数回、オペラ座の私の専用ボックス席が、他の人間に使われていたのだ。私は前支配人

the opera was filled by somebody else. I wrote to the old managers, Mr. Debienne and Mr. Poligny, to ask them to please explain. They replied by saying they had shown you the rule book and told you about my demands. So, I must assume that you are choosing not to respect my wishes.

Let me be clear: If you value your own safety, you must not take away my private box! I wish to see Christine Daae perform, and if I cannot do this from Box Five, you and other members of the opera will pay dearly.

Yours Truly,
Opera Ghost

When they were finished reading, the managers looked at each other. This joke seemed to be going too far. They decided to call in the box-keeper to their office to ask exactly what she knew about Box Five.

Mrs. Giry, the mother of the little dancer Meg Giry, soon came to the office. She was an older lady with gray hair and an old, black dress.

■respect 動 ～に配慮する　■value 動 ～を尊重する　■take away 奪う　■pay dearly 多大の犠牲を払う　■Yours Truly, 敬具　■go too far 度が過ぎる　■box-keeper 名（劇場などの）ボックス席係

のドビエンヌ氏とボリニー氏に手紙を書いて、説明を求めた。すると2人は、職務規定書をあなたがたに見せ、私の要求も伝えたと答えてきた。つまり、あなたがたが私の願いをあえて無視したと思わざるを得ない。

　はっきり言わせてもらおう。もし自分の身が大事なら、私の専用ボックス席を奪ってはならない！　私はクリスティーヌ・ダーエの演技を観たいと願っている。もし5番ボックス席から観ることができなければ、あなたたちもオペラ座の他の者たちも、大きな犠牲を払うことになるだろう。

敬具
オペラ座の怪人

　支配人たちは読み終わって、互いに顔を見合わせた。いくらジョークとはいえ、これはやり過ぎではないか。そこでボックス係を支配人室に呼び、5番ボックス席について知っていることをはっきり尋ねることにした。

　小さな踊り子のメグ・ジリーの母親、ジリー夫人が、まもなく支配人室へやってきた。かなり年配の白髪の女で、古ぼけた黒い服を着ていた。

"How may I help you, sirs?" she asked.

"Mrs. Giry, you are the box-keeper, are you not? You know all the guests who own private boxes?"

"Yes, sir."

"Well, tell us about the guest who owns Box Five."

Mrs. Giry suddenly looked worried and didn't say anything.

"Well? What have you to say?" Mr. Richard demanded.

"I don't like to talk about Box Five, sir."

"Why not?"

"Because—because it's not good luck, sir. The owner of that box is the opera ghost."

"That's what I thought!" said Mr. Richard. "And who is this ghost exactly?"

"Why, I've never seen him! But I hear him. He thanks me when I put his program in the box."

"How is it that you don't see him but you do hear him?"

"Well ... He's a ghost, sir."

Mr. Richard was getting angry.

"Isn't there anything you can tell us that is of some use?" he cried out.

■How may I help you? どのようなご用件でしょうか？　■exactly 副 一体全体
■why 間 あら、まあ　■be of some use ひとかどの役に立つ

「なんのご用でしょうか？」と、彼女は聞いた。

「ジリーさん、あなたはボックス係でしたね？ 専用ボックス席の客のことは全員ご存じですかな？」

「ええ、存じております」

「それでは、５番ボックス席の客について話してください」

ジリー夫人はたちまち不安そうな顔つきになって、何も言おうとしなかった。

「おや？ 答えてくれないのですか？」リシャール氏が返答を求めた。

「５番ボックス席のことは話したくないんです」

「どうして？」

「だって——縁起が悪いからですよ。あのボックス席はオペラ座の怪人のものなんです」

「そんなことだと思った！」とリシャール氏。「で、この怪人とはいったい何者なんです？」

「あら、私は見たことありませんよ！ でも、声は聞こえます。ボックス席にプログラムを置くと、ありがとうって言うんです」

「見えないのに声が聞こえるとは、どういうことです？」

「それは……まあ、幽霊ですからね」

リシャール氏は腹が立ってきた。

「もっと役に立つことが話せないのかね？」と、彼は怒鳴った。

Mrs. Giry didn't like being talked to in this way. She stood up taller and put her nose in the air.

"I believe I've answered your questions to the best of my ability, sir," she said.

Mr. Moncharmin stepped in quickly.

"Dear Mrs. Giry," he said. "Don't mind Mr. Richard. He does not know how to speak to a lady." Here he threw an angry look at Mr. Richard.

"Please, if there is anything else you know about the guest who 'owns' Box Five, be so good as to tell us."

Mrs. Giry seemed to soften a bit.

"Well, I can tell you that the ghost likes to cause trouble when he doesn't get what he wants. For example, one night, when Mr. Poligny and Mr. Debienne were still quite new, they made the mistake of putting three guests in Box Five. It was Mr. and Mrs. Maniera—you know, they own that jewelry store in the center of town—and their friend, Mr. Isidore Saack. Well, when the show started, there was a great love scene. While the actors on stage were kissing, a voice whispered in Mr. Maniera's ear, 'Ha ha! Julie wouldn't mind giving a kiss to Isidore!' Mr. Maniera turned to his wife, Julie, and he saw that Mr. Saack was kissing her hand!

■put one's nose in the air つんと上を向く　■throw an angry look at ～を怒りの目で見る　■soften 動（心などが）穏やかになる　■make a mistake ミスをする　■not mind よい、構わない

ジリー夫人はこのような言い方をされたのが気に入らなかった。そこで、すっくと立ち上がり、鼻先をつんと上に向けた。
「私は、あなたの質問に精一杯答えたと思いますよ」と、彼女は言った。

　モンシャルマン氏がすばやく割って入った。
「これはどうも、ジリーさん。リシャールさんのことは気にしないでください。ご婦人への言葉づかいというものを知らないのですよ」と言って、リシャール氏をにらみつけた。
「お願いです。もし５番ボックス席を『持っている』客について、他に知っていることがあるなら、どうか教えてください」
　ジリー夫人は少し気を取り直したようだった。
「そうですねえ、怪人は欲しいものが手に入らないと、問題を起こすのが好きなんですよ。たとえば、ある晩、ポリニーさんとドビエンヌさんがまだ新任の頃に、間違って５番ボックス席に３人のお客さんを入れたことがありましてね。マニエラ夫妻——ほら、街の真ん中に宝石店を持ってる方ですよ——それから、お友だちのイジドール・サックさんです。劇が始まって大事なラブシーンがありました。俳優たちが舞台でキスをしていると、マニエラさんの耳にささやく声がしたんです。『ハハハ！　ジュリーはイジドールにキスしてもいいそうだぞ！』って。それでマニエラさんが奥さんのジュリーの方を見ると、サックさんがその手にキスしてたんですよ！

Well, the two men started fighting! As Mr. Saack ran away, he fell down the grand staircase and broke his leg! It will be a long time before he can walk up those stairs again, I'm sure."

There was a quiet moment as the managers thought about this story.

"You have been very helpful, Mrs. Giry," said Mr. Moncharmin. "Thank you very much for your time. You are free to go."

When Mrs. Giry had left the room, the two managers turned to each other.

"I am not at all impressed," said Mr. Richard firmly. "That story doesn't prove anything about any ghost."

"Quite right," said Mr. Moncharmin. "Let's forget about this ghost! He is nothing but an old wives' tale."

With that, the managers went about their business.

■run away 逃げ出す　■break one's leg 足を骨折する　■I'm sure. 違いありません。
■free to 自由に〜できる　■not at all 少しも〜でない　■be nothing but ただ〜にすぎない

男たちのけんかが始まりました！　サックさんは逃げる時に大階段を転げ落ちて、足の骨を折ったんです！　あの階段をまた上れるようになるには、きっとずいぶん時間がかかりますよ」

　部屋はしんと静まりかえり、支配人たちはこの話についてしばらく考えていた。

「とても助かりましたよ、ジリーさん」とモンシャルマン氏。「お時間を取ってくれて、どうもありがとう。もう行って結構ですよ」

　ジリー夫人が部屋を出ていくと、2人の支配人は顔を見合わせた。

「私はなんとも思わないぞ」と、リシャール氏が断固として言った。「あんな話、怪人についてのなんの証拠にもならんよ」

「そのとおりだ」とモンシャルマン氏。「怪人のことは忘れよう！　年寄りの夫人のたわごとにすぎないさ」

　そして、支配人たちは仕事に戻った。

5. In Perros

Meanwhile, Christine Daae did not give any more wonderful performances at the opera. She went back to being good but not *great*. She even turned down a few offers to perform at parties and shows. People tried to guess why she hid from attention. I believe the reason was fear. Christine was afraid of her own excellence, and she was afraid of what had happened to her that evening that she performed as Margarita.

She did not go out, and she didn't reply to any of Raoul's letters until one morning, she wrote him this note:

Dear Sir,

I have not forgotten the little boy who went into the sea to save my scarf. I felt I had to write to you today, before I go to Perros. Tomorrow is the anniversary of my father's death. You knew my father, and he liked you very much.

■go back to（元の状態に）戻る　■turn down（依頼などを）断る　■guess 動 推測する　■anniversary of someone's death（人）の命日

5. ペロスにて

　一方、クリスティーヌ・ダーエはオペラ座で、もうそれほど素晴らしい演技を見せようとはしなかった。悪くはないが、月並みな歌手に戻ってしまった。パーティーやショーで歌ってほしいという数件の依頼さえ断った。なぜ注目されまいとするのか、人々はいろいろと憶測した。きっと恐れが原因だったのだろう。クリスティーヌは自分の優れた才能が怖かった。そして、マルガリータを演じた夜に自分の身に起こったことを恐れていたのだ。

　彼女は外に出ようとせず、ラウルの手紙にも返事さえしなかったが、ついにある朝、ラウルに次のような手紙を書いた。

　　拝啓

　私は、スカーフを取りに海へ入ってくれた少年のことを忘れてはいません。今日ペロスへ行く前に、やはりお手紙を差し上げなくてはと思ったので、書くことにしました。明日は父の命日です。私の父をご存じでしたわね。父はあなたのことが大好きでした。

He is buried in Perros with his violin, by the little church. It is at the bottom of the hill where we used to play as children—the same place we said goodbye for the last time.

After reading this letter, Raoul caught the first train to Perros. As he traveled, he remembered the story of the little Swedish singer and her father.

There was once a poor man named Daae who had a little daughter, Christine. They lived in Sweden until Daae's wife passed away. Christine was still very young at the time. With no money or land, Daae brought Christine to the sea-side town of Perros, France, for a chance at a better life.

Many people believed Daae was the best violin player in all of France—some believed in all the world. His daughter also had the voice of an angel, and the two would stand together on the street and perform some of the most beautiful music anyone had ever heard.

One summer, a little boy who was to grow up to become the Viscount of Chagny came to Perros with his aunt. This boy was, of course, Raoul.

■catch a train 列車に飛び乗る ■Swedish 形 スウェーデンの ■there was once かつて~があった[いた] ■pass away 死去する

父はペロスの小さな教会のそばで、自分のヴァイオリンと一緒に眠っています。その教会は、私たちが子どもの頃によく遊んだ丘のふもとにあります——最後にさようならを言った、あの同じ場所です。

この手紙を読んで、ラウルはペロス行きの始発列車に飛び乗った。その車中で、スウェーデンの幼い歌手と父親の物語に思いを馳せていた。

その昔、クリスティーヌという小さな娘を持つ、ダーエという名の貧しい男がいた。スウェーデンに住んでいたが、やがてダーエの妻が亡くなった。当時クリスティーヌはまだとても幼かった。金も土地もなかったダーエは、もっとよい暮しができるかもしれないと、フランスの海辺の町ペロスへ、クリスティーヌを連れてやってきた。

多くの人が、ダーエはフランスで一番のヴァイオリニストに違いないと思った——中には、世界一だと信じる者もいた。娘も天使のような声をしていたので、２人は一緒に通りに立ち、それまで誰も聞いたことがないほど美しい音楽を演奏したものだった。

ある夏のこと、やがて成長してシャニー子爵となるべき少年が、叔母とともにペロスの町へやってきた。その少年とは、もちろんラウルである。

For young Raoul, it was love at first sight. He followed Christine and her father to the sea, where they went walking one afternoon. The wind was strong that day and blew Christine's scarf into the sea.

"Don't worry, Miss," said Raoul. "I'll get your scarf for you!"

He ran straight into the sea. When he returned the scarf to Christine, she was so happy that she kissed him. His aunt, meanwhile, was not very happy.

From that day, Christine and Raoul were great friends. They spent many hours playing together and listening to Daae's stories. Their favorite story was about the Angel of Music. Whoever the Angel of Music visited on earth would become a musical genius. Daae told Christine that he would send her the Angel of Music someday, once he had died and gone to heaven.

Finally, when Raoul had to leave Perros, he and Christine said goodbye at the bottom of the hill where they often played.

"I shall never forget you!" Raoul said.

■love at first sight 一目ぼれ　■whoever 代 〜な人なら誰でも　■once 接 〜次第すぐに

年若いラウルにとって、それは一目ぼれだった。ある日の午後、ラウルはクリスティーヌとその父親について海へ行き、一緒に散歩をしていた。その日は風が強かったので、クリスティーヌのスカーフが海へ飛ばされてしまった。
　「大丈夫です、お嬢さん」とラウル。「ぼくがスカーフを取ってきます！」

　ラウルはまっすぐ海の中へ走っていった。ラウルからスカーフを受け取った時、クリスティーヌはとてもうれしくて彼にキスをした。その一方で、ラウルの叔母は不機嫌だった。
　その日から、クリスティーヌとラウルは大の仲良しになった。2人は何時間も一緒に遊んだり、ダーエの話を聞いたりして過ごした。お気に入りは音楽の天使の話だった。音楽の天使が地上の人間を訪れると、その人は必ず音楽の天才になれるという。ダーエは、いつか死んで天国へ行ったら、音楽の天使をクリスティーヌのもとへ送ろうと約束した。

　そしてとうとう、ラウルがペロスを去らねばならない日がやってきた。ラウルとクリスティーヌは、よく遊んだ丘のふもとで別れの挨拶を交わした。

　「君のことは決して忘れないよ！」ラウルが言った。

Christine had tears in her eyes as he walked away. Raoul, too, felt like crying, for he knew that a poor girl like Christine could never be the wife of the Viscount of Chagny.

As the years passed, Christine often thought of Raoul and continued to sing. However, when her father died, she seemed to lose her voice. She sang well enough to get into music school, where she did not shine but did well enough to become a part of the Paris Opera. Raoul knew this and had come to see her perform when he returned to Paris. However, he was surprised to find that she did not sing as well as she once did. In fact, since her father's death, nobody heard the true quality of her voice until the night she sang as Margarita. That night, it was as if she was Christine Daae again, the girl with the voice that could make angels cry.

Suddenly, the train came to a stop. Raoul had arrived in Perros. He asked the workers at the station if they had seen a Parisian woman with long, golden hair. They told him that they saw a woman with hair like that go to the Setting Sun Inn that day. Raoul hurried there.

Raoul opened the door of the Setting Sun to find Christine sitting there. She was smiling and waiting for him.

■feel like doing ～したい ■part of ～の一員 ■ask someone if ～かどうかを(人)に尋ねる ■Parisian 形 パリ風の ■inn 名 宿

ラウルが歩き去っていく時、クリスティーヌは目に涙をためていた。ラウルも泣きたい思いだった。彼女のように貧しい娘が、シャニー子爵の妻になることなどありえないからだ。

　それから数年が経ち、クリスティーヌはラウルの面影を胸に抱きながら歌い続けた。だが父親が死んだ時、自分の声を失ったように感じた。音楽学校に入れる程度には歌えたが、目立つほどではなく、それでもパリ・オペラ座の一員にはなれた。ラウルはこのことを知り、パリへ戻ると、彼女の演技を観にやってきた。だが彼女が昔のように歌えないことを知って、ラウルは驚いた。それどころか、父親の死後、誰もクリスティーヌの本物の声を聞いたことがなかった。そう、マルガリータとして歌ったあの夜までは。その夜、彼女は天使をも泣かせる声の少女、クリスティーヌ・ダーエに再び戻ったようだった。

　突然、列車が止まった。ペロスに着いたのだ。ラウルは駅員に、長い金髪のパリ風の女を見なかったか尋ねた。駅員たちは、その日、そういう髪型の女が夕陽荘の方へ行くのを見たと答えた。ラウルはその宿屋へ急いだ。

　ラウルが夕陽荘のドアを開けると、そこにクリスティーヌが座っていた。彼女は微笑んでいた。ラウルを待っていたのだ。

"Hello, my old friend," she said. "I'm glad to see you here."

"Christine! Finally, you speak to me!" said Raoul. He rushed toward her and took her hands. Then, his feelings took over and Raoul spoke angrily.

"Why did you not reply to any of my letters? Why did you not recognize me before? Haven't you ever seen me at the opera? I even followed you to your room several times, but you acted like you never saw me!"

Christine turned red.

"Yes, I had seen you," she said.

"Why did you never speak to me? Don't you know that I love you?"

"Please, don't be foolish," said Christine, turning away. "You can't love a poor opera girl like me."

"Do you love someone else?" demanded Raoul. "I heard a man's voice in your room that night! That night you fainted," he said.

Suddenly, Christine looked at him with fear.

"Whose voice?" she demanded.

■take over 取って代わる　■turn red 赤くなる　■demand 勵問いただす

「こんにちは。私の懐かしいお友だち」彼女は言った。「ここでお会いできてうれしいわ」

「クリスティーヌ！　ああ、やっと、ぼくに話しかけてくれたね！」ラウルは彼女に走り寄り、その手を取った。すると感情があふれてきて、怒ったように話しだした。

「どうしてぼくの手紙に一度も返事をくれなかったんだい？　どうして前はぼくがわからなかったんだ？　オペラ座でぼくを見かけたことはなかったのかい？　何度か君の楽屋までついていったことさえあるんだよ。なのに、君はぼくに会ったことがないふりをして！」

クリスティーヌは顔を赤らめた。

「ええ、あなたを見かけたことがあるわ」と、彼女は言った。

「だったら、なぜ話しかけてくれなかったんだ？　愛しているのがわからないのかい？」

「お願いだから、ばかなことを言わないで」とクリスティーヌは言って、顔を背けた。「私みたいな貧しいオペラ歌手を、あなたが愛せるわけないわ」

「他に好きな人がいるのか？」ラウルは、きつい調子で尋ねた。「あの夜、君の楽屋で男の声が聞こえたんだ！　君が失神したあの夜だよ」

すると突然、クリスティーヌはおびえた顔でラウルを見つめた。

「誰の声ですって？」彼女は強い口調で尋ねた。

"The man who said, 'You must love me, Christine!' Then you said you had given your soul to him! He replied, 'Your soul is a beautiful thing.'"

Christine put a hand over her heart. She sat down and was still for a long time. Finally, she looked at Raoul.

"I ... I have a secret," she said. "Do you remember my father telling me that he would send me the Angel of Music after he died? Well, he has died, and he has sent him to me!"

"What do you mean?"

"That voice you heard in my room that night—it's him. The Angel of Music comes to me in my dressing room every day. I never see him, but I can hear him. I didn't know anyone else could hear him, but you heard him too!"

"If you're joking, stop this. I don't like it," said Raoul.

"I'm telling the truth, Raoul!" said Christine. "The Angel of Music teaches me how to sing, and he says I will become the greatest singer in the world!"

■still 形 じっとした、動かない　■anyone else 他人

「男の声だよ。『君は私を愛さねばならない、クリスティーヌ！』と言っていた。それから君が、魂を彼に捧げたと言ったんだ！　すると男が『君の魂は美しい』と答えた」

　クリスティーヌは胸に手を当てた。そして座りこみ、長い間じっとしていた。それからやっと、ラウルの方を見た。

　「私……秘密があるの。あなた覚えてる？　父が、自分が死んだら音楽の天使を私に送ると言っていたでしょう。父は亡くなったわ、そして、あの人を私に送ってくれたの！」

　「どういう意味だい？」

　「あの夜、私の部屋であなたが聞いた声よ——それがあの人なの。音楽の天使が、私の楽屋に毎日やってくるのよ。姿を見たことはないけど、声が聞こえるの。他の人にも聞こえるなんて知らなかったわ。でも、あなたにも聞こえたのね！」

　「冗談ならよしてくれ。そういうのは好きじゃない」とラウル。

　「本当の話なのよ、ラウル！」とクリスティーヌ。「音楽の天使が、歌い方を教えてくれてるの。そして、私は世界一偉大な歌手になれるって言うのよ！」

6. *Faust* and What Followed

In the following weeks, the managers of the opera sold tickets to Box Five with no regard to the threats of the opera ghost. They decided to end the whole idea of the ghost once and for all. They let everybody know that on Saturday evening, when *Faust* was to be performed, the managers themselves would sit in Box Five to watch the show.

But, on Saturday, as the managers settled into their seats, they seemed worried. They looked at each other, not quite knowing what to expect. However, as the first act ended without any problems, they began to feel relief. They even started joking to each other, saying, "Has anybody whispered in your ear yet?"

The second act also came and went with no problems. The managers were quite happy now and laughed quietly to themselves as they watched the show.

■with no regard to ～などお構いなしに ■once and for all きっぱりと ■act 名（劇などの）幕 ■feel relief 安心する

6.『ファウスト』とその後

　その後の数週間、オペラ座の支配人たちは、オペラ座の怪人の脅しなどお構いなしに、5番ボックス席の切符を販売した。彼らは怪人説そのものに終止符を打とうと決心していた。そこで、土曜日の夜の『ファウスト』上演時に、支配人たち自らが5番ボックス席で観劇すると、皆に通告した。

　それでも、土曜日になって席に着いたとき、支配人たちのようすは不安気だった。何を予期しているのかわからないまま、互いに顔を見合わせていた。しかし第1幕が問題なく終わったので、2人は安心しはじめた。冗談さえ交わすようになってきた。「もう誰かが耳にささやいてきたかね？」

　第2幕も問題なく始まり、無事に進んでいった。今や支配人たちはたいへんご機嫌で、静かにほくそ笑みながら劇を観ていた。

Carlotta made her entrance as Margarita and sang her first few lines. The rest of the act went beautifully. After the act ended, there was a short intermission, and the managers went out of the private box to talk for a few minutes. When they returned to their seats, they found a box of chocolates there.

"That's strange," said Mr. Moncharmin. "Who could have brought those in here?"

They settled back into their seats to watch the rest of the show. Also watching just a few boxes down were Raoul and Philippe de Chagny. They had come to see Christine Daae, who was playing the part of Siebel in *Faust*. However, Christine's singing was off that night, and she was causing more than one person in the audience to whisper, "What is wrong with that girl? One night she sings like an angel, and the next night she sounds like some singer off the street!"

Philippe was angry—he had written to the managers of the opera to praise Christine. Knowing that his brother, Raoul, loved Christine, he had hoped to advance her position at the opera. He had put his good name on the line for her, yet this is how she performed? How dare she!

■line 名（劇などの）せりふ、節　■intermission 名（劇などの）幕間、休憩時間　■settle back into ～に身を沈める　■off 形 調子が悪い　■more than one person 複数の人　■What is wrong with ~ ?　～は一体どうしたのですか？　■off the street 街角で　■advance 動 ～を昇進させる　■how dare よくも～できるものだ

マルガリータに扮したカルロッタが登場し、最初の数節を歌いだした。残りの場面も素晴らしい進行ぶりだった。その幕が終わると短い幕間があったので、支配人たちは専用ボックス席を出て数分話をした。そして席へ戻った時、チョコレートの箱があるのに気づいた。

「おや、変だな」とモンシャルマン氏。「誰がこんなものを持ってきたんだろう？」

　支配人たちは椅子にゆったりと腰かけて、劇の続きを観た。少し下のボックス席では、ラウルとフィリップ・ド・シャニーも観劇していた。クリスティーヌ・ダーエを観に来たのだ。彼女は『ファウスト』でジーベルの役を演じていた。しかし、その夜のクリスティーヌの歌は芳しくなかったので、観客の何人かがささやいた。「あの子はどうなってるんだ？　ある夜は天使のように歌い、次の夜には街角の歌い子のような有様とは！」

　フィリップは怒っていた――オペラ座の支配人たちに、クリスティーヌをほめる手紙を書いていたからだ。弟のラウルがクリスティーヌを愛していると知り、オペラ座での地位を上げてやりたいと思ったのである。彼女のために立派な署名さえしてやったというのに、今夜の歌いぶりはどうだ？　よくこんなことができるものだ！

Raoul, on the other hand, was quietly crying. He could not bear to watch Christine. She had lost all her cheer, all her vivacity! It made him sad—sadder than the letter he had received from her the day before. It had read:

My dear friend,

You and I must never see each other any more. If you truly love me, please do this for me. My life and your life depend on it.

Your Christine

Now, on the stage, Carlotta was singing her finest. She was getting to the most beautiful part of Margarita's song. As she threw back her shoulders and smiled wide for the crowd, she opened her mouth and this is the sound that came out:
"Co-ack!"
There was a moment of shock. Carlotta blinked a couple of times in wonder, then shook off the strange event. She opened her mouth, and again she sang, "Co-ack!"

■vivacity 图快活　■throw back one's shoulders 胸を張る　■co-ack 图クワック《ヒキガエルのような鳴き声》　■blink 動まばたきする

一方、ラウルは声を殺して泣いていた。そんなクリスティーヌを見ていられなかった。元気さも快活さもすべて失っている！　そのことが彼には悲しかった——前日に受けとった彼女の手紙よりも悲しかった。手紙にはこう書かれていた。

　　大切なお友だちへ

　　私たちはもう会ってはいけないのです。私を本当に愛しているのなら、どうか私のためにそうしてください。私の命も、あなたの命も、それにかかっているのですから。

　　　　　　　　　　　　　　　　　　　　　あなたのクリスティーヌより

　今、舞台では、カルロッタがこれ以上ないほど見事な声で歌っていた。マルガリータの歌のもっとも美しい箇所が近づいてきた。カルロッタは胸を張り、観客に晴れやかな笑顔を向けて口を開いた。すると、そこから出た音はこれだった。
「ゲコッ！」
　衝撃の一瞬だった。カルロッタは当惑して数回まばたきをし、このありえない事態を振り払おうとした。そして口を開いて、もう一度歌ってみた。
「ゲコッ！」

The audience went wild.

"What kind of show is this? Is she sick? What's happened?"

Carlotta tried again and again to control her voice, but she only sang, "Co-ack! Co-ack! Co-ack!"

It was hopeless. Her voice had gone, and Carlotta stood on the stage in total shock. The guests filling the opera house cried out in anger. Surely, this was not what they had paid good money to see!

In Box Five, the managers turned white and closed their eyes. The opera ghost had struck! He was laughing at them! Then, very clearly, they heard a voice close to them say, "She is singing tonight to bring down the chandelier!" Then Box Five filled with his laughter.

Suddenly, the managers looked to the ceiling where the huge glass chandelier was hanging. In a moment, before anyone could do anything, the chandelier came crashing down to the floor below. As people ran, the voice kept laughing.

The newspaper the next day reported that many had been hurt and one person had been killed by the chandelier. People reading the newspaper thought to themselves, "The opera must be cursed."

■go wild 大騒ぎする　■good money 大金　■struck 動strike（襲いかかる）の過去・過去分詞　■bring down 墜落させる　■curse 動 〜に呪いをかける

観客は騒然となった。
「なんだ、この劇は？　具合でも悪いのか？　いったい何があったんだ？」
　カルロッタは何度も声を整えようとしたが、この音しか出なかった。「ゲコッ！　ゲコッ！　ゲコッ！」
　もうどうしようもない。カルロッタは声を失い、すっかり動転して舞台に突っ立った。オペラ座に満員の観客たちが、怒りの声をあげた。たしかに、こんな芝居を観るために大枚をはたいたのではないのだ！

　５番ボックス席では、支配人たちが顔色を失い、目を閉じた。オペラ座の怪人の仕業だ！　我々を笑っているのだ！　そのとき、とてもはっきりと、すぐそばで声がした。「今夜のカルロッタの歌声には、シャンデリアも落ちそうだな！」そして５番ボックス席に怪人の笑い声が響き渡った。

　はっとして、支配人たちは、巨大なガラスのシャンデリアがぶらさがる天井を見上げた。そのとたん、誰も何もできないうちに、シャンデリアが床に落ちて粉々に砕け散った。人々が逃げまどうなか、あの笑い声がいつまでも響いていた。

　翌日の新聞は、シャンデリアの落下によって大勢が怪我をし、１人が亡くなったと報じた。新聞を読みながら人々は心の中で思った。「オペラ座は呪われているに違いない」と。

覚えておきたい英語表現［文法］

敬意をあらわす英語表現

基本文法をおさらいすると、読みが確実になります。物語を楽しみながら、合わせて文法力もつけましょう。ここでは、丁寧さに注目して、手紙の文面や会話から敬意をあらわすための英語表現を復習しましょう。

> I'm sorry to trouble you during this busy time. （p.50, 下から3行目）
> お忙しいところをお邪魔して申し訳ない。

【解説】怪人から新しい支配人へ向けた初めての手紙ですので、まずは敬意を表してこう始まっています。「お忙しいところご面倒をおかけして申し訳ありません」と言いたいときに、ビジネスのメールでも、日常の場面でも、そのまま使えますから、覚えておくと便利です。もうすでに迷惑をかけてしまったときは、「to + have + 過去分詞」という完了形の不定詞を使ってあらわすことができます。

【例文】　I'm extremely sorry to have troubled you.
ご迷惑をおかけしてしまい、誠に申し訳ありません。

　troubleは「〜に面倒をかける、迷惑をかける」と言う意味の他動詞ですが、troubleを名詞として使うこともできます。

【例文】　It's a lot of trouble.
それ面倒なんです。

　　　　That company is in trouble.
その会社はトラブルの中にある→経営難に陥っている。

> However, I had to bring to your attention something very important. (p.50, 下から3行目)
> しかしながら、大変重要なことを指摘しなければならなくなった。

【解説】前の1文、I'm sorry to trouble you … に続く文です。ビジネスレターで使えそうな表現は、bring + O + to one's attention「〜にOを伝える」です。上の文では、目的語である something very important が後に来ているので、文の構造がわかりにくくなっています。I had to tell you something very important. と言っても意味は同じですが、文面に威厳を持たせるために、もったいぶった言い方になっています。ふだんの会話で言うことはありませんが、クレームのメールなどにも使えそうですね。

【例文】 There is something I would like to bring to your attention.
お伝えしておきたいことがあります。

I am writing to you on behalf of the residents of the condominium to bring to your attention a liquefaction-related matter.
マンションの住民を代表して、液状化に関することで申し上げたいことがあり、お手紙を差し上げた次第です。

> You and other members of the opera will pay dearly.
> (p.52, 8行目)
> あなたたちもオペラ座の他の者たちも、大きな犠牲を払うことになるだろう。

【解説】dearly は「高い代償を払って (at a high cost)」、will pay dearly は「高い代償を払うことになるだろう」と脅しています。先ほどの sorry を使って、You'll be sorry about this later.「後で後悔するぞ」も使えますが、いずれにせよ、脅していることに違いないので、will pay dearly とカッコつけても、かなりきつい表現であることはかわりません。

【例文】 You will pay dearly for this.
こんなことをすると罰が当たりますよ→このツケは大きいぞ。

> Dear Mr. Manager, ... Yours Truly, (p.50, 下から4行目)
> 拝啓　支配人殿　　　　　　敬具

【解説】同じく怪人が支配人に宛てた手紙の冒頭、salutation（冒頭礼辞）と結びのことばです。ビジネスレターのでは、相手の役職名を用いて Dear Manager, とするのがふつうです。ここでは Mr. Manager とわざわざ敬称をつけていて、ちょっと奇妙な印象を受けます（Mr. President や Mr. Chairman などと、役職名に敬称をつけて呼びかけに使われることはあります）。結びの礼辞も Sincerely yours, より改まった Yours Truly, で終っています。慇懃無礼な感じが出ています。

> Dear Sir, (p.60, 下から5行目)
> 拝啓

【解説】これはクリスティーヌがラウルに宛てた手紙の salutation（冒頭礼辞）です。まだ、彼女がラウルと距離をとっていたときなので、Dear Sir, とフォーマルでよそよそしい言い方になっています。Dear Sir, は、もともと相手の名前がわからないときに使っていましたが、最近のビジネスレターでは Dear Manager, のように、役職名を使うことが多いようです。個人的な手紙ではもちろん Dear Miss Daae, や Dear Christine, のように個人名を入れます。

　ペロスでふたりが会った後にクリスティーヌがラウルに出した手紙は、My dear friend, で始まり、Your Christine で結んでいて、親密さが表現されています。第7章で仮面舞踏会の前にラウルのもとに届いた手紙は、My dear Raoul, で始まりますが、結びは Christine（とおそらくサイン）だけで、緊迫した様子が見てとれます。

> Please, if there is anything else you know about the guest who 'owns' Box Five, <u>be so good as to</u> tell us. (p.56, 9行目)
> お願いです。もし5番ボックス席を「持っている」客について、他に知っていることがあるなら、どうか教えてください。

【解説】これは、支配人 Mr. Richard の無礼な物言いに腹を立てたボックス係のMrs. Giry に対して、もう一人の支配人 Mr. Moncharmin がとりなすように、あらためて丁重に質問したことばです。(Please) be so good as to ～で「お手数ですが～してください」と依頼する表現ですが、少し古くさく聞こえるかもしれません。

本文では、Please と be so good as … の間に、if there is anything else you know …, と条件節が挿入されて、さらに丁寧な言い回しになっています。

一方、Mr. Richard のことばは、次のようにぶっきらぼうな命令口調で、ぶしつけな詰問調です。

"Well, tell us about the guest who owns Box Five." (それでは、5番ボックス席の客について話してください)

"Well? What have you to say?" (おや？ 答えてくれないのですか？)

"And who is this ghost exactly?" (で、この怪人とはいったい何者なんです？)

"How is it that you don't see him but you do hear him?" (見えないのに聞こえるとは、どういうことです？)

"Isn't there anything you can tell us that is of some use?" (もっと役に立つことが話せないのかね？)

ストレートな表現は、言い方によっては失礼になることがあるのは、日本語も同じですね。

【例文】 Would you <u>be so good as to</u> lend me some money?
いくらかお金を貸してくださいませんか。

<u>Be so good as</u> to follow me.
私のあとについてきていただけますか。

Part 3

7. The Masked Ball

That terrible event was bad for everyone. Carlotta fell ill. Christine disappeared. She was not seen or heard of for ten days after the performance. Then, one morning, as Raoul sat in his bedroom lost in sad thoughts, his servant brought him a letter.

Raoul recognized the paper and writing. He tore open the letter and read,

My dear Raoul,

Go to the masked ball at the opera tomorrow night. At twelve o'clock, be in the little room behind the grand staircase and stand by the door. Wear a white cape and mask. Do not let yourself be recognized.

Christine

■fall ill 病気になる ■lost in thought もの思いにふける ■servant 名召使い
■tore 動tear（破る）の過去 ■ball 名舞踏会

7. 仮面舞踏会

　その恐ろしい事件は、あらゆる人に悪い結果をもたらした。カルロッタは病床についた。そしてクリスティーヌが行方不明になった。その公演後の10日間、姿も音沙汰もなかったのだ。しかしある朝、ラウルが寝室で悲しくもの思いにふけりながら座っていると、召使いが1通の手紙を持ってきた。

　ラウルはその用紙と筆跡に見覚えがあった。破って開け、手紙を読んだ。

　大切なラウルへ

　明日の夜、オペラ座の仮面舞踏会に来てください。12時に、大階段の後ろの小部屋に入って、入口のそばに立つのよ。白いマントと仮面をつけて。あなただとわからないようにしてくださいね。

　　　　　　　　　　　　　　　　　　　　　　　　クリスティーヌ

Raoul wondered what all this was about, and he was getting quite tired of such strange letters. Christine seemed strange all the time—first acting as if she didn't know him, then telling him to come to Perros. Then she had told him that story of the Angel of Music coming to her dressing room. Raoul did not know what to make of that. It was all too strange, but his heart called out for Christine. That day, he bought a white cape and mask. The next night, Raoul went to the ball.

The opera was filled with people. Making his way through the guests, Raoul found the little room behind the grand staircase. Although the room was crowded, by twelve, he had found some space to stand by the door. Suddenly, a woman in a black cape and mask came toward him and touched his arm. She walked out the door without a word and Raoul followed. It was Christine!

As they made their way through the ball, Raoul didn't even notice the wonderful dress clothes of the guests. However, there was one man he did notice: He was dressed all in red, with a long, red cape that dragged on the ground behind him. He walked proudly like a king, but his face was a perfect death's head! His eyes, nose, and mouth were four

■get tired of ～にうんざりする ■what to make of ～をどう判断するか ■call out for ～を大声で呼ぶ ■make one's way through ～の間を通り抜ける

これはいったいどういうことだろう。ラウルはもう、そのような不可解な手紙にはうんざりだった。クリスティーヌはいつも不可解だ——はじめは彼を知らないかのようにふるまい、その後でペロスへ来るように言う。それから、音楽の天使が楽屋に来るという、あの話だ。どう判断したらいいのか、まるでわからない。すべてはあまりにも不可解だ。それでも心はクリスティーヌを求めて叫んでいた。その日、ラウルは白いマントと仮面を買った。そして翌日の夜、舞踏会へと向かった。

　オペラ座は人であふれていた。ラウルは客たちの間をすり抜けて、大階段の後ろの小部屋を見つけた。部屋は混んでいたが、12時までには、入口のそばに立つすき間を見つけることができた。するといきなり、黒いマントに仮面の女が彼に近づいて腕に触れた。そして一言も言わずにドアを出たので、ラウルは後についていった。あれはクリスティーヌだ！

　舞踏会の中を通り抜けていく間、ラウルは客たちの素晴らしい衣装に気づきさえしなかった。だが、1人だけ目を引く男がいた。その男は全身赤い衣装で身を包み、床に引きずるほど長くて赤いマントを羽織っていた。王のように誇らしく歩いていたが、その顔はまさしくどくろだった！　目と、鼻と、口は、4つの黒い穴。マントには金文字で「触れるな！　私はさまよう〈赤い死〉だ！」と書かれている。

black holes. On his cape were the gold words, "Do not touch me! I am Red Death walking!"

Everybody was very impressed with Red Death. Some skilled artist must have created that wonderful death's head! Some guests even followed Red Death around. But Raoul noticed as they moved through the opera that Red Death seemed to be following him and Christine.

Raoul followed Christine up the stairs to a private box. She kept looking over her shoulder. Before she shut the door of the private box behind them, she heard footsteps on the stairs. Quickly she looked out the door and saw a red foot on a stair, then a red leg—

"It is he!" she whispered and shut the door.

"Is that the man who you sing for and you give your soul to?" said Raoul. "That man dressed as Red Death is your Angel of Music? Well, I have something to say to him. I'll tear off his mask and tear off my own, and we'll speak to each other honestly, like men, and see who really loves you!"

Raoul tried to open the door but Christine blocked his way.

■impress 動 ～を感心させる ■skilled 形 熟練した ■follow someone around （人）の後をついてまわる ■look over one's shoulder 後ろを振り返る ■tear off ～をはぎ取る

皆、〈赤い死〉の仮装にとても感心した。どこかの巧みな芸術家が、あの見事などくろを作ったに違いない！　客の中には、〈赤い死〉の男についてまわる者さえいた。だがラウルは、自分とクリスティーヌがオペラ座の中を移動する間、〈赤い死〉が後をつけてきているらしいと気づいた。

　ラウルはクリスティーヌについて階段を上がり、ボックス席へ向かった。彼女はつねに後ろを振り返っていた。ボックス席に入ってドアを閉めようとした時、階段に足音がした。すばやくドアの外をのぞくと、階段に赤い足先が見え、やがて赤い脚が現れて——

「あの人だわ！」クリスティーヌはささやいて、ドアを閉めた。
「あの男か？　君が歌って魂を捧げたという、あの男なのか？」とラウル。「〈赤い死〉の姿をした男が、音楽の天使だって？　じゃあ、その男に言いたいことがある。そいつの仮面をはぎとり、ぼくのもはがそう。率直に、男らしく話し合って、どちらが本当に君を愛しているかはっきりさせるんだ！」

　ラウルはドアを開けようとしたが、クリスティーヌがそれを阻んだ。

"You must not!" she cried. "Please, my love, please do not go out there!"

Raoul suddenly stopped.

"Christine," he said, "did you say 'my love'?"

It was the first time he had heard her say that she loved him.

"Yes, dear," she said. "And if you love me too, you must never be seen or recognized by *him*."

She reached out her hands to Raoul, and he noticed she was wearing a gold ring on her finger.

"Christine!" cried Raoul. "Did *he* give you that? How can you tell me you love me, but wear his ring?"

Christine's hands dropped.

"I have to," she said sadly, "or terrible things will happen. You will never understand *his* sadness, or mine. He will hurt people, including you, if I do not go live with him."

She removed her mask, and Raoul saw the deep sadness on her face.

■out there 向こうに　■reach out 〜を差し出す　■remove 動(衣服などを)脱ぐ

「だめよ！」と、彼女は叫んだ。「お願い、愛しいあなた、お願いだから出ないで！」

ラウルはふと動きを止めた。

「クリスティーヌ」とラウル。「『愛しいあなた』って言ったかい？」

彼女からラウルへの愛の言葉を聞いたのは、それが初めてだった。

「ええ、そうよ」とクリスティーヌ。「そしてあなたも私を愛しているなら、ぜったいにあの人に見られたり、知られたりしないでちょうだい」

クリスティーヌはラウルに手を伸ばした。すると、その指に金の指輪がはめられていることに、ラウルは気がついた。

「クリスティーヌ！」ラウルは悲痛な声をあげた。「あの男にもらったのか？ その指輪をはめながら、ぼくを愛しているなんて、よく言えるね？」

クリスティーヌは手を下ろした。

「はめなきゃいけないの」と、悲しそうに言った。「でないと、恐ろしいことが起こるのよ。あなたには、あの人の悲しみも、私の悲しみもきっとわからないわ。あの人は、私が一緒に生きていかなければ、あなたもみんなも傷つけるつもりなのよ」

クリスティーヌが仮面を取ると、その顔に深い悲しみが宿っているのをラウルは見た。

"Christine!" he cried. "What do you mean you have to live with him? What have you done?"

"My love," she said, "please, let us be happy together for this one month. I know you will leave Paris to go sailing again in four weeks. Before you go away, can we be secretly engaged? *He* will be working for the next month. But when he is done working, he will come for me. Our month of happiness will be over ... but it will have been the best time of my life!"

Raoul got on one knee in front of her. He hardly knew what he was doing, and he didn't understand everything she was saying, but there was nothing more he wanted than to be married to this singer whom he had loved all his life.

"Christine," he said, "may I have your hand in marriage?"

She put her hand into his and said happily, "You already have it!"

■done 形 終わった　■hardly 副 ほとんど～でない　■all one's life 一生を通じて
■have someone's hand in marriage 結婚する

「クリスティーヌ！」と、彼は声をあげた。「あの男と一緒に生きていかなければならないって、どういう意味だい？　いったい何をしたんだ？」
　「愛しいあなた」とクリスティーヌ。「お願い、この１か月は、一緒に幸せに過ごしましょう。あなたが４週間後にはパリを去って、また航海に出ることを知ってるわ。行ってしまう前に、秘密の婚約をしない？　あの人は来月、仕事をするつもりなの。でもそれが終わったら、私のところへ戻ってくるわ。私たちの幸福なひと月はそれで終わり……でも、きっと私の人生で最高のひとときになるわ！」

　ラウルはクリスティーヌの前で片ひざをついた。自分が何をしているのかよくわからず、また彼女の言葉の意味も全部は理解できなかった。だが、彼が何よりも望んでいるのは、命をかけて愛しているこの歌手と結婚することだった。
　「クリスティーヌ」とラウル。「結婚していただけますか？　さあ、その手をぼくに」
　彼女は自分の手をラウルの手に重ね、幸せそうに言った。「とうにあなたのものよ！」

8. Above the Trap-Doors

So began Christine and Raoul's month of happiness. She called for him to come to her dressing room most nights at the opera. On days they did not see each other, they wrote letters. This was also the high point of Christine's career as a singer. Angry about her terrible performance, Carlotta had canceled her contract and Christine had taken her place. After signing the contract, Christine had disappeared for two whole days, but when she came back, she sang like never before. She won over everyone at every performance. It was as if some angel had touched her and given her a voice from heaven.

Raoul was filled with joy every time he visited Christine in her dressing room. One day, however, she did not notice he was at her door. Raoul saw her looking sadly into her mirror and saying softly, "Poor Erik … Poor Erik."

■contract 名契約　■take someone's place（人）の代わりをする　■win over（演技などで）〜を魅了する　■poor 形かわいそうな

8. 隠し戸の上で

　そのようにして、クリスティーヌとラウルの幸福なひと月が始まった。クリスティーヌは、ほとんど毎晩オペラ座の楽屋へラウルを呼んだ。会えない日には、手紙を書きあった。この時期はまた、クリスティーヌは歌手としても最高潮だった。カルロッタが自分の失態に憤怒して契約を解除したので、クリスティーヌがあとを引き継いだのだ。契約を結んだ後、クリスティーヌは丸２日間姿を消したが、戻ってくると、今までとは別人のような歌いぶりになっていた。あらゆる演技で、あらゆる人を魅了した。まるで天使が彼女に触れて、天国の声を授けたかのようだった。

　ラウルは、クリスティーヌに会いに楽屋へ行くたびに、喜びで満たされた。しかしある日、ラウルが戸口にいることに彼女は気づかなかった。そして悲しげに鏡をのぞき、そっとこう言ったのだ。「かわいそうなエリック……かわいそうなエリック」

Raoul felt a rush of anger—he was sure this was the name of Christine's Angel of Music.

"But I'll show her how happy we are together," thought Raoul, "and make her forget all about this 'Erik.' He won't take her from me again!" With that, he walked into her room with a smile, as if he had seen and heard nothing.

Christine and Raoul often walked throughout the opera—all seventeen floors of it, behind, over, and under the stage, in all the hidden corners and secret halls. One day, Raoul saw an open trap-door in the floor and looked down into the darkness below.

"You've taken me all through the opera, Christine, but you've never taken me to the world below. I know there are many cellars. Shall we go?"

But, shaking and with eyes wide with fear, Christine pulled him away from the trap-door and said, "No! No! Everything underground belongs to *him*!"

When she said this, the trap-door suddenly shut. She pulled Raoul away, saying there were much nicer things to see on top of the roof, in the sun and among the birds. As she led him away, she looked over her shoulder. However, she didn't see the shadow that followed her.

■trap-door 名隠し戸、落とし戸 ■below 副階下に ■pull someone away（人）を引き離す ■roof 名屋上 ■lead someone away（人）を連れて行く

ラウルは怒りがこみ上げるのを感じた——きっとクリスティーヌの音楽の天使の名前だ。
「いや、ぼくといることがどれほど幸せか、彼女にわからせてやろう。そして、『エリック』という男のことはすっかり忘れさせるんだ。そんなやつに二度と渡すものか！」そう考えて、ラウルは何も見聞きしていないかのように、笑顔で部屋に入った。
　クリスティーヌとラウルは、よくオペラ座の中を歩いてまわった——17階建ての建物の各階、後ろ側、外側、舞台下、そしてあらゆる隠れた隅や秘密の廊下などを見た。ある日、ラウルは床の隠し戸が開いているのに気づき、その下の暗闇をのぞきこんだ。

「君はオペラ座じゅうを案内してくれたね、クリスティーヌ。でも、まだ地下には連れていってくれていないよ。地下室がたくさんあることは知ってるんだ。さあ、行こうか？」
　ところが、クリスティーヌは震えながら恐怖で目を見開き、ラウルを隠し戸から引き離した。「だめ！　だめよ！　地下はすべて、あの人のものなの！」
　そう言ったとたん、隠し戸がいきなり閉まった。彼女はラウルをそこから引き離し、屋上なら日が差し小鳥たちもいて、もっといいものが見られると言った。ラウルを連れていきながら、彼女はうしろを振り返った。しかし、後をつけてくる人影は見えなかった。

9. Erik

Christine led Raoul to the roof, and there they saw all of Paris below them. It was just around sunset, and they sat down together for a while. But soon, Christine started to shake and seemed very worried.

"What is it, my love?" asked Raoul gently.

"Dear, I feel I must tell you everything. Here, on the roof, we are as far away from *him* as we can be. Our time together is running out, and before we part, I must let you know the truth."

Then, Christine began to tell her story.

"I called him 'the voice' before I knew his name was Erik," she said. "About three months ago, when I was in my dressing room, I heard a beautiful voice. It was singing, and I had never heard anything like it. I looked out into the hall and in all the rooms near mine, but nobody was there. So I had a foolish idea.

■run out 時間切れになる　■part 動 別れる　■look out into ～を眺める

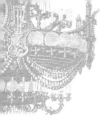

9. エリック

　クリスティーヌがラウルを屋上につれていくと、眼下にパリを一望することができた。ちょうど日が沈むころで、2人はしばらく一緒に座っていた。しかしまもなく、クリスティーヌが震えだして、とても不安そうな顔つきになった。
「どうしたんだい、愛しいクリスティーヌ？」と、ラウルがやさしく聞いた。
「ねえ、すべてお話しするべきだと思うの。この屋上なら、あの人からできるだけ離れていられるわ。2人の時間はもうすぐ終わり。お別れする前に、本当のことを言わなくては」
　そして、クリスティーヌは話を始めた。
「あの人の名前がエリックだとわかる前は、『声』と呼んでいたの」と彼女は言った。「3か月ほど前のことよ。楽屋にいたら、美しい声が聞こえてきたの。歌っていたんだけど、今までそんな声を聞いたことがなかったわ。私は廊下や、近くの部屋を全部のぞいてみたけれど、誰もいなかった。それで、ばかげたことを考えてしまったの。

"My father told me he would send me the Angel of Music when he died. Well, my poor father died, and I waited, but the angel never came. So I called out to the voice, 'Are you my Angel of Music whom my father has sent to me?'

"'Yes!' it replied.

"Since then, the voice and I became great friends. We talked every day. Then the voice asked if it could give me music lessons. I said yes. The voice taught me so many wonderful things, and I found that I could sing like never before. But I kept it a secret because the voice, my teacher, told me it was not time to show the world yet.

"One day, I recognized you, dear, at the opera. You must have just returned to Paris from your travels. I was so happy to see you that I told the voice about you. But the voice became quiet. I called out to it again and again but it didn't reply. I was afraid it had gone forever.

"The next night, the voice came back. I was so happy it had not left me! It said I was ready to let the world hear the music of heaven. That night, Carlotta fell ill and I gave my best performance. I sang so hard it was as if my soul were leaving me. It was beautiful, but I was also afraid of it all! I fainted, and when I woke, I saw you.

■whom 関 ～するところの人　■ask if ～かどうか尋ねる　■time to do ～すべき時期　■again and again 何度も

父は、自分が死んだら音楽の天使を送ると言っていたわ。そのうち、かわいそうな父が亡くなって、私は待っていたけれど、天使はやってこなかった。だから、声に呼びかけてみたの。『あなたは、父が送ってくれた音楽の天使なの?』って。
　『そうだよ』と、声は答えたわ。
　それから、声と私はとても仲よくなったの。毎日お話したわ。そのうち、声が音楽を教えてあげようかって聞いてきた。私は、ええ、と答えたの。声は素晴らしいことをたくさん教えてくれたわ。気がつくと、私は以前とは見違えるほど歌えるようになっていたの。でも、先生の声が、まだ世間に見せる時ではないと言うから秘密にしていたのよ。

　そんなある日、オペラ座であなたを見つけたの。きっと旅を終えてパリに戻ってきたところだったのね。会えてとてもうれしかったから、声にあなたのことを話したわ。でも声は黙りこんだの。何度も呼んだけれど返事がなくて。もう永遠に消えたのかと心配したわ。

　でも翌日の夜、声は戻ってきた。消えてしまったのではないとわかって、とてもうれしかったわ!　声は私に、そろそろ世間に天国の音楽を聞かせてもいい頃だと言ったの。その夜にカルロッタが病気になって、私は最高の演技をしたのよ。あまりに一生懸命に歌ったから、魂が抜けていきそうだったわ。素晴らしかったけれど、同時に何もかもが怖かったの!　それで気を失って、目が覚めたら、あなたがいたのよ。

9. エリック

"I knew the voice was there, so I acted like I didn't recognize you. Even so, the voice continued to be jealous, saying bad things about you every day. I got tired of it and I told the voice, 'That's enough. I'm going to Perros tomorrow and I'm going to ask Raoul to come with me.' The voice said that was fine, but if I married anyone on earth, he would leave me forever.

"Then, on the night that the chandelier fell, I was so afraid for you and the voice. I knew you were safe because I saw you in your brother's box. I thought if the voice was safe too, he would probably be in my dressing room. I ran there and called out to the voice. Suddenly, I can't explain how, but I heard the voice singing and my mirrors doubled and opened. When I walked toward it, I was suddenly outside of my room!

"It was dark and cold. The singing had stopped. A man in a black cape appeared and held me tightly. I struggled, but he put his hand over my mouth. His hand smelled like death! I fainted, and when I awoke, I was in a boat on an underground lake. The man with the black cape was taking me somewhere. He wore a mask that covered his whole face.

■act 動 ふるまう　■even so それでも　■fine 形 よい、構わない　■be afraid for 〜を気遣う　■struggle 動 もがく

声がそこにいるのを知っていたから、あなたがわからないふりをしたのよ。それでも、声は嫉妬しつづけて、毎日あなたの悪口を言ったわ。わたしはうんざりして、声に言ったの。『もうたくさん。私は明日ペロスへ行くわ。そしてラウルも誘うつもりよ』って。そしたら声は、よかろう、だが地上の誰と結婚しようと永遠に離さないぞ、と言ったのよ。

　そしてシャンデリアが落ちたあの夜、私はあなたと声のことがとても心配だったわ。でも、あなたがお兄さまのボックス席にいるのが見えたから、無事だとわかった。もし声も無事なら、楽屋にいるだろうと思ったから、楽屋に走っていって呼びかけたの。そのとたん、ああ、うまく説明できないけれど、声の歌うのが聞こえて、鏡が二つ折りになって開いたの。それに向かって歩いていくと、あっという間に部屋の外に出たのよ！

　そこは暗くて寒かったわ。歌はもう止んでいた。黒マントを着た男が現れて、私を強く抱き締めたの。もがいたけれど、男は私の口の上に手を置いた。その手は死人のような匂いがしたわ！　気が遠くなって、目が覚めたら、地下湖で舟に乗っていたのよ。黒マントの男が、私をどこかへ連れていくところだったの。男は顔全体を仮面で隠していたわ。

"We finally came to a bright place. It was a house on the edge of the lake! The man finally spoke. He said, 'Don't worry Christine, you're safe here.' It was the voice!

"I was angry and I cried out, 'Why have you brought me here? What do you want with me?' The voice just said, 'Come, I have something to show you.' He must have given me some drug because I followed.

"First, he showed me a lovely bedroom. He said this was where I would stay. Then he showed me his bedroom … Oh, it was terrible! The walls were all black, with music notes written all over them. A huge organ covered one entire wall. And his bed … his bed was a coffin!

"I was very afraid. 'Who are you?' I asked. He took me into a living room then, and he sat me down. Then, he fell at my feet and told me he was sorry!

"'I'm sorry, Christine,' he said. 'I lied. I'm not your Angel of Music. I'm not even a ghost. I'm just a man, and my name is Erik. This is where I live, Christine, and I love you! I want you to stay with me!'

■edge of 〜のふち ■music note 音符 ■entire 形 全体の ■coffin 名 棺桶 ■fall at one's feet （人）の足元にひざまずく

私たちはようやく明るい所に着いた。湖畔の家よ！　男がとうとう口を開いたわ。『心配いらないよ、クリスティーヌ。ここなら安全だ』って。それは、あの声だったのよ！

　私は怒って叫んだわ。『どうして私をここへ連れてきたの？　何が望みなの？』って。でも声は、『おいで、見せたいものがある』と言うだけだった。きっと、私が従うように薬を飲ませたのね。

　最初に、すてきな寝室を見せてくれたわ。これが私の泊まる部屋だって。それから、あの人の寝室も……ああ、恐ろしかったわ！　どの壁も真っ黒で、一面に音符が書かれていた。それと、壁が隠れるほど大きなオルガン。そしてベッドは……ベッドは棺だったわ！

　私はとても怖かった。『あなたはいったい誰なの？』と聞いたわ。すると、あの人は私を居間へ連れていって座らせたの。それから、私の足元にひざまずいて、あやまったのよ！

　『すまない、クリスティーヌ』と言ったわ。『私はうそをついていた。私は君の音楽の天使ではない。怪人でさえない。ただの人間で、名前はエリックだ。ここに住んでいる。そして、クリスティーヌ、君を愛しているのだ！どうか一緒にいておくれ！』

"I suppose you will be angry with me, Raoul, but in that moment I pitied him. A man, living all alone under the opera, and with such a beautiful voice that no one knows about—how sad and lonely his life must be!

"I asked him to take off his mask, but he refused. Then, when he wasn't expecting it, I reached out and pulled his mask away! Oh! It was horrible, Raoul, horrible!"

"What, Christine? What did you see?"

"Erik is a living dead man! He has a death's head—his eyes, nose, and mouth are four large black holes! He was so angry that I saw his face that he grabbed me by my hair and pulled me into my room—"

"Enough!" cried Raoul, his heart in pain.

"—and he ran into his room, shut the door, and began to play the organ. The song was beautiful and frightening at the same time! It made everything at the opera seem like child's play. It expressed every human emotion possible. I later found out it is called *Don Juan Triumphant*. It is Erik's masterpiece.

■pity 動 〜に同情する　■all alone ただ一人で　■take off（衣服などを）脱ぐ　■pull something away（物）をもぎ取る　■grab someone by（人）の〜を引っつかむ　■find out 知る　■masterpiece 名 傑作

あなたはたぶん怒るでしょうね、ラウル。でもそのとき、私はあの人がかわいそうになったの。オペラ座の地下にひとりぼっちで住んで、あんなに美しい声をしているのに誰にも知られることもない人——その人生は、どんなに悲しくて寂しいことでしょう！

　私は、仮面を取ってと頼んだけれど、断られたわ。でも、ふいをついて手を伸ばし、仮面を引きはがしたの！　ああ！　恐ろしい！　ラウル、とてもひどかったわ！」

　「なんだい？　クリスティーヌ、何を見たんだい？」

　「エリックは生ける屍なのよ！　どくろの顔で——目と、鼻と、口が４つの大きな黒い穴なの！　あの人は顔を見られたことにとても腹を立てて、私の髪をつかむと、私の部屋へ引きずっていったわ——」

　「もうたくさんだ！」ラウルは胸が痛み、思わず叫んだ。

　「——それからエリックは自分の部屋へ走っていって、ドアを閉め、オルガンを弾きはじめた。その曲は美しくて、同時にぞっとするほど怖かったわ。オペラ座の劇が、すべて子どもの芝居のように思えるほどよ。人間が持ちうるあらゆる感情を表現していたわ。後でわかったことだけど、『勝ち誇るドンファン』という曲なの。エリックの傑作よ。

"I was afraid, but the music took hold of me. I rose and slowly walked to his room. I opened the door and watched him play. He was crying. I said to him, 'Erik! Show me your face without fear! You are the most unhappy of men, but you are a genius of music! If I ever look at you and have to turn away, it is not because of your face. It is because I am thinking of your pure genius!'

"He slowly turned to me then, for he believed me. It was a terrible sight—a skull crying. But I went to him, and I touched his arm. He stopped playing and he fell at my feet with words of love.

"And so it went, for the next ten days. We sang together almost all the time. The music was the most beautiful I have ever heard, but of course I cannot love him! I acted like I was happy, and after the tenth day, he told me I could be free, as long as I came to visit him often. He gave me this gold ring, and showed me the way out of the underground house on the lake."

Christine put her arms around Raoul as she finished her story.

■take hold of（心などを）とらえる　■if I ever do　仮に〜することがあるとしたら　■and so it goes　このようにして　■as long as　〜さえすれば　■put one's arms around　〜の体に腕を回す

怖かったけれど、その曲に私は心をつかまれたの。立ち上がって、ゆっくりとエリックの部屋へ向かったわ。ドアを開けて、オルガンを弾く様子を見ていたの。あの人は泣いていた。私はこう言ったの。『エリック！　怖がらずに顔を見せて！　あなたほど不幸な人はいない。でも音楽の天才だわ！　あなたを見て顔を背けなければいけないとしたら、それは顔のせいじゃない。あなたが全くの天才だと思うからよ！』

　すると、あの人はゆっくりと振り向いた。私を信じてくれたのね。恐ろしい光景だった——どくろが泣いていたの。でも私は近づいて腕に触れたわ。あの人は弾くのをやめ、私の足元にひざまずいて、愛していると言ったの。

　そんなふうにして10日間が過ぎた。ほとんどいつも一緒に歌っていたの。その音楽は聞いたことがないほど美しかったけれど、もちろん、あの人を愛することはできないわ！　でも幸せそうなふりをしたから、10日後には、度々会いに来るなら自由にしてもいいと言われたの。そしてこの金の指輪を渡して、地下湖の家から出る道を教えてくれたのよ」

　クリスティーヌは話し終えると、ラウルの体に腕をまわして抱いた。

"We must run away tonight," Raoul said, holding her tightly. "We must leave Erik for good!"

"We cannot," she said simply. "Erik has let me go, but only for now. A few days after I returned to the opera, Erik's voice came and spoke to me in my dressing room. He said he knew I loved you, but he also knew that you were going away in a month. He said he loved me so much he could not bear to be without me. He said I could spend a month together with you if I came to live with him afterward. He said he would spend this month working on *Don Juan Triumphant*, and when he was done, we would marry! If I didn't agree to this, he said, he would do terrible things to my friends!"

Christine looked into Raoul's eyes.

"You see? I cannot hate Erik, because I pity him. Nobody has ever loved him. But he is truly a monster, and I must do as he says!"

"No, Christine, he is not your master!" said Raoul. "I will help you leave him! You will live the life you want! You want to be with me, don't you?"

■for good 永遠に ■bear 動 我慢する ■afterward 副 あとで ■work on 〜に取り組む

「今夜一緒に逃げるんだ」ラウルは彼女を強く抱きしめて言った。「エリックから永遠に離れなければ！」

「できないわ」と、彼女はぽつりと言った。「エリックは私を放してくれたけど、今だけなのよ。オペラ座に戻った数日後に、楽屋でエリックの声が話しかけてきたの。あの人は、私があなたを愛していることも、あなたが１か月後にいなくなることも知っていると言ったわ。そして、私をとても愛しているから、私なしでは生きられないって。もし後であの人と一緒に暮らすなら、１か月間あなたと過ごしてもいいと言うの。今月は『勝ち誇るドンファン』の作曲に取り組むから、それが完成したら結婚するんだって！もし断ったら、私の大切な人たちに恐ろしいことが起こると言ったのよ！」

クリスティーヌはラウルの目をのぞきこんだ。

「わかった？　私はエリックを憎めない。かわいそうですもの。あの人は誰にも愛されたことがないのよ。でも本物の怪物だわ。なのに言うとおりにしなくちゃいけないの！」

「だめだ、クリスティーヌ、あいつは君の主人じゃない！」とラウル。「ぼくがあいつから離してあげるよ！　自分の望むように生きるんだ！　ぼくと一緒にいたいんだろう？」

"Yes, I love you!" said Christine. "I would do anything to be with you. Yes, you're right! Let's leave this place forever! But I can't leave now—it would kill him if I left now. Let him hear me sing tomorrow. After the performance, at midnight, you must come and take me away!" Christine grew excited and her eyes shone. "At midnight, you must take me away from here!"

The young lovers held each other close. They did not notice the shadow behind them, which had heard every word.

■do anything 何でもやる ■take someone away（人）を連れ出す ■hold someone close（人）をギュッと抱きしめる

「そうよ、愛してるわ！」とクリスティーヌ。「あなたといるためなら、なんでもするわ。そうね、あなたの言うとおりよ。ここから永遠に出ていきましょう！　でも、今はだめ——今行ったら、あの人は死んでしまう。明日私の歌を聞かせてあげるわ。公演が終わったら、真夜中に迎えにきて！」彼女は興奮して瞳を輝かせた。「真夜中に、ここから連れ出してちょうだい！」

　若い恋人たちは、しっかりと抱き合った。その後ろに人影があり、一言漏らさず聞いていたことを、2人は知らなかった。

覚えておきたい英語表現［文法］

比較級と最上級、比喩表現

基本文法をおさらいすると、読みが確実になります。物語を楽しみながら、合わせて文法力もつけましょう。ここでは、比較の使い方に注目です。比較級や最上級を使うと気持ちがこもります。as if … と like … など、比喩を使ってイメージを具体的に説明することができます。

> but there was <u>nothing more</u> he wanted <u>than</u> to be married to this singer whom he had loved all his life. (p.94, 12行目)
> だが、彼が何よりも望んでいるのは、命をかけて愛しているこの歌手と結婚することだった。

【解説】「nothing + 比較級 + than ～」で「～より…なものはない」、つまり「～が一番…」と最上級の意味を表わす表現です。He wanted to be married to this singer. と言っている内容は同じでも、伝わる気持ちの強さは全然違います。
　I'd like to marry you. より I'd like nothing better than to marry you.（君と結婚できるなら何もいらない）と言われた方が、嬉しくないですか。marry ～は「～と結婚する」。be married to ～は「～と結婚している」という状態と「～と結婚する」という動作を表わすことができます。

　ちなみに、本文ではこの後、次のようなラウルのことばが続きます。

"Christine," he said, "may I have your hand in marriage?"
（「クリスティーヌ、結婚していただけますか？」）

もともと、"May I have your daughter's hand in marriage?"（お嬢さんを僕にください）という伝統的な言い回しがあります。男性が花嫁の父親に結婚の許しを請うときの表現ですが、ここでは、ラウルがクリスティーヌに直接言っているので、May I have your hand in marriage? となっています。古風な言い方ですが、貴族の青年らしさが出ています。クリスティーヌの答えは "You already have it!"（とうにあなたのものよ！）

【例文】 There is nothing better than drinking beer on a hot summer day.
暑い夏の日にビールを飲むのは最高です。

Nothing is more important than your health.
健康ほど大切なものはない。

nothing の代わりに「no (other) + 単数名詞」を使って、「no (other) + 単数名詞 + 比較級 + than〜」というパターンを応用すれば、言えることがもっと広がります。

【例文】 No one in the world is happier than I am.
私ほど幸せな人は世界にいない→私が世界で一番幸せ。

The music was the most beautiful I have ever heard. (p.110, 13行目)
その音楽は聞いたことがないほど美しかった。

【解説】「the + 最上級 + (that) + 主語 + 完了形」のパターンで、「これまで…した中で一番〜」、つまり「今まで…したことがないほど〜」と最上級の意味を強めることができます。

【例文】 This is the most thrilling movie (that) I have ever seen.
これは私が今まで見た中で一番はらはらする映画だ。

Christine made her entrance in the second act, and her voice was more beautiful than ever. (p.122, 8行目)
クリスティーヌは第2幕に登場し、その声は今までにないほど美しかった。

【解説】比較級と than ever を組み合わせると「かつてないほど〜」つまり「今までで一番〜」と最上級の意味を表します。

【例文】 He has got broader powers than ever.
彼はこれまでにないほど広い権限を得た。

Young people feel more insecure than ever before.
若者はこれまでになく不安を感じている。

as〜as ever は「これまでと同じくらい〜」という意味、as〜as ever lived は「きわめて〜」という意味になるので注意。

【例文】 She is as beautiful as ever.
彼女は相変わらず美しい。

Erik is as great a singer as ever lived.
エリックは今まで存在したどんな偉大な歌手と較べても劣らない偉大な歌手だ→きわめて偉大な歌手だ。

余談ですが、第9章p.113で、ラウルがクリスティーヌに「今夜一緒に逃げるんだ」と言った次のセリフ "We must leave Erik for good!"（エリックから永遠に離れなければ）の for good は for ever (forever) の意味です。

> I sang so hard it was as if my soul were leaving me.
> （p.102, 20行目）
> あまりに一生懸命に歌ったから、魂が抜けていきそうだったわ。

【解説】「so〜that … 」で「非常に〜なので…」という構文ですが、上の文は hard と it の間に that が省略されています。as if は「あたかも…するかのように」。実際は魂が抜け出ることはないので、were leaving と仮定法過去が使われています。主節の動詞が現在形でも過去形でも、主節の動詞と同じ時のことであれば、仮定法過去を使い、それより前のことなら仮定法過去完了形を使います。

【例文】 He cares for the cat as if she were his child.
彼はわが子のようにその猫を世話する。

Tokyo Skytree Tower looked as if it touched the clouds.
東京スカイツリーは雲に届いているかのように見えた。

話し手が事実とは異なる空想だと思っていれば、仮定法を使います。

【例文】 Christine looks as if she saw a ghost.
クリスティーヌはあたかも幽霊を見ているかのようだ。

Christine looks as if she had seen a ghost.
クリスティーヌはあたかも幽霊を見たかのようだ。

話し手が事実だろうと思っていれば、直接法を使います。

【例文】　Christine talks <u>as if</u> she <u>is</u> angry.
　　　　クリスティーヌは怒っているみたいな口ぶりだ。

> It was <u>as if</u> some angel <u>had touched</u> her and <u>given</u> her a voice from heaven. (p.96, 9行目)
> まるで天使が彼女に触れて、天国の声を授けたかのようだった。

【解説】天使が彼女に触れたわけでも、天国の声を授けたわけでもないので、as if 節では had touched, (had) given と仮定法過去完了が使われています。

> With that, he walked into her room with a smile, <u>as if</u> he <u>had seen and heard</u> nothing. (p.98, 5行目)
> そう考えて、ラウルは何も見聞きしていないかのように、笑顔で部屋に入った。

【解説】実際は、ラウルはクリスティーヌが鏡に向かって「かわいそうなエリック」と言っているのを聞いてしまいました。事実とは違いますので、ここでも had seen and heard nothing と仮定法過去完了が使われています。そろそろ仮定法の使い方に慣れてきましたでしょうか。仮定法とは、事実とは異なることを言うときの「動詞の形」のことです。

> I knew the voice was there, so I acted <u>like</u> I didn't recognize you. (p.104, 1行目)
> 声がそこにいるのを知っていたから、あなたがわからないふりをしたのよ。

【解説】話し言葉では、as if 同様、like も接続詞として、「あたかも…するかのように」という意味を表します。

【例文】　It seems <u>like</u> it will rain today.　今日は雨が降りそうだ。
　　　　Do I look <u>like</u> I'm joking?　僕が冗談を言っているようにみえますか。
　　　　You look <u>like</u> you've seen a ghost.　幽霊でも見たみたいだね。

119

パリの地下空間

His hand smelled like death! I fainted, and when I awoke, I was in a boat on an underground lake. (p.104, 下から4行目)

「パリの地下に湖？」と疑問に思われるかもしれませんが、実はパリの地下には広大な地下空間が広がっています。これは採石場の跡。ノートルダム寺院をはじめ、パリの荘厳な街並みをかたち作る数々の建造物は、パリの地下から掘り出された良質の石灰岩からできているのです。採石は19世紀まで続き、その跡は、250キロも続く地下の迷宮（labyrinth）となって、華やかなパリの街の足元に広がっています。地下の世界には、水路や貯水池、集会場やワインセラーなど、あらゆるものがあります。巨大な共同墓地（カタコンブ）も。この地下墓地には600万体の遺骨が納められていて（体の部位毎に、きちんと積み上げられています）、世界最大の地下墓地となっています。

複雑な地下の空間は、第2次世界大戦でパリがドイツに占領されたときには、レジスタンスの隠れ家にもなりました。パリにあったグランモスクでは、イスラム教徒が命がけでユダヤ教徒をかくまい、地下の通路を通って安全な郊外へと逃がした記録が残っています。

1955年からは地下への無断の立ち入りは禁じられていますが、1970年代から80年代にかけては、自由を求める若者たちによる、芸術、ドラッグなどの「地下活動」が盛んになりました。現在は多くの入り口が閉鎖されたため、「活動」は下火となりましたが、それでも「カタフィル」とよばれる地下愛好家たちが自由を楽しむ場となっているようです。

ちなみに、前述の地下墓地（カタコンブ）は観光ツアーで見学することができます。ミュージカルの曲の一節、"And in this labyrinth where night is blind" が聞こえてくるようです。

Part 4

10. Christine! Christine!

The next day, Raoul secretly prepared to leave Paris with Christine. A horse and carriage, money, food, extra clothing, and hired help were all ready by nine o'clock at night. By then, it was time to go to the opera.

That night, the opera was showing *Faust*. Raoul settled into his private box with his brother, Count Philippe de Chagny.

The first act was splendid. Christine made her entrance in the second act, and her voice was more beautiful than ever. People felt like they were listening to the angels singing in heaven.

Then, at the most moving part of *Faust*, Christine held out her arms and sang the words, "My spirit longs to be with you!"

■carriage 图大型四輪馬車　■extra 形余分の　■clothing 图衣類　■than ever かつてないほどに　■moving 形感動的な　■hold out one's arms 両手を差しのべる
■long to ～することを切望する

10. クリスティーヌ！ クリスティーヌ！

　翌日、ラウルは密かに、クリスティーヌとともにパリを去る用意をした。馬と馬車、金、食料、着替、そして雇人など、夜の9時までにすべて準備が整うことになっていた。その前に、オペラ座へ行く時間がやってきた。

　その夜、オペラ座は『ファウスト』を上演していた。ラウルは兄のフィリップ・ド・シャニー伯爵とともに専用ボックス席に着いた。

　第1幕の演技は素晴らしかった。クリスティーヌは第2幕に登場し、その声は今までにないほど美しかった。人々は、天国の天使の歌を聞いているように感じた。

　そして、『ファウスト』のもっとも感動的な場面で、クリスティーヌは両手を前に差しだしてこの歌詞を歌った。「どうか私の魂を、あなたとともにいさせてください！」

Suddenly, the opera went totally dark. The music stopped. Then, just as suddenly, the lights came back on. But Christine Daae was not on the stage!

The singers and actors looked at each other in shock. Guests began to whisper to each other, "What is this? Surely this isn't part of the show?"

Suddenly, one by one, everyone in the opera realized that Christine had disappeared and she wasn't coming back!

The whole opera went wild. Raoul jumped from his seat and ran to his carriage waiting outside. The carriage was still there, but it was empty—no Christine! What had happened? Where had she gone? Had that monster Erik taken her?

Raoul looked all around him in a fit of madness.

"Christine!" he cried out. "Christine!"

It took a while for Raoul to calm down and think clearly. He finally realized the best thing to do was to go to the managers and see if they knew anything. At the managers' office, he was met by the police chief, who had rushed to the opera as soon as he learned that a singer had disappeared.

■go dark 暗くなる　■one by one 一人ずつ　■in a fit of madness 気が狂ったように　■it take a while 少し時間がかかる　■see if ～かどうか確かめる

すると突然、オペラ座全体が真っ暗になった。音楽も止んだ。その後、やはり突然に明かりがついた。ところが、クリスティーヌ・ダーエは舞台にいなかった！

　歌手や俳優たちが驚いて顔を見合わせた。観客たちが互いにささやき始めた。「これはなんだ？　たしか劇中にこんな場面はなかっただろう？」

　次の瞬間、1人また1人と、オペラ座じゅうの人たちが、クリスティーヌが消えたまま戻らないことに気づいたのだ！

　オペラ座全体が騒然となった。ラウルは椅子から跳び上がり、外に待たせた馬車へ走っていった。馬車はまだそこにあったが、中は空っぽだった——クリスティーヌがいない！　何が起こったんだ？　彼女はどこへ行った？　あの怪物エリックが連れ去ったのか？

　ラウルは狂ったように、そこらじゅうを見まわした。

「クリスティーヌ！」と大声で叫んだ。「クリスティーヌ！」

　落着いてまともに考えられるようになるまで、しばらくかかった。ようやく、支配人たちに何か知らないか聞きに行くのが一番だと気づいた。支配人室に着くと、警察署長に出会った。歌手が消えたという知らせを受けて、すぐオペラ座に駆けつけたのだ。

10. クリスティーヌ！　クリスティーヌ！

In the office, Raoul told the managers and the police chief the story of Erik, his underground house by the lake, and his terrible love for Christine.

"He has her, I know it! We must go under the opera, but how do we get there? Please, you must tell me how!"

Both managers looked at each other and the police chief just stared at Raoul. Nobody said anything.

"Well? Can you help me?" asked Raoul.

"Dear Viscount," the police chief finally said, "you were planning on running away with Christine after the show tonight, correct?"

"Yes, sir."

"And you had a carriage ready for this?"

"Yes, sir."

"And did you notice whose carriage had drawn up next to yours tonight?"

"No, sir.

"It was your brother's. And did you notice that his carriage is now gone?"

■police chief 警察署長　■get there そこに到達する　■draw up（車などを）止める

支配人室で、ラウルは支配人たちと警察署長に、エリックのことや、地下湖の家、そしてクリスティーヌに対するエリックの恐ろしいまでの恋情について話した。

「あいつが連れ去ったんだ、ぼくにはわかります！　オペラ座の地下へ行かなければ。でもどうやって行くのですか？　お願いです、行き方を教えてください！」

　両支配人は顔を見合わせ、警察署長はラウルをじっと見つめるだけだった。誰も何も言わなかった。

「どうしたんです？　助けてくれないんですか？」ラウルは聞いた。

「子爵殿」警察署長がとうとう口を開いた。「今夜の上演が終わったら、あなたはクリスティーヌと逃げるつもりだった、そうですね？」

「はい、そうです」

「そして、そのために馬車を用意していた？」

「はい」

「それでは、今夜あなたの馬車の横に、誰の馬車が停められていたかお気づきでしたか？」

「いいえ」

「あなたの兄上の馬車ですよ。では、その馬車が今はないことはご存じですかな？」

"No, sir."

"I believe that your brother has taken Christine with him. Perhaps he didn't agree to your marriage. Perhaps he loved her too! Either way, Christine is gone, and so is your brother, Count Philippe de Chagny."

"Philippe!" cried out Raoul. "I will find him!"

He jumped up and ran out the door. His mind was racing, and again, he was not thinking clearly. But as soon as he began to run down the hall, he was stopped by a strange man. He had dark skin and green eyes that shone. Raoul had seen him at the opera before. He tried to think who it was … It was the Persian!

"Viscount of Chagny," said the Persian, "I know the monster named Erik. I believe he has taken Christine, and I think I can help you save her!"

■either way どちらにしても　■race 動 疾走する

「いいえ」

「きっと兄上がクリスティーヌを連れ去ったのでしょう。おそらく兄上はあなたのご結婚に反対だった。たぶん彼もクリスティーヌを愛していたからですよ！　いずれにせよ、クリスティーヌも、あなたの兄上、フィリップ・ド・シャニー伯爵もいなくなったのです」

「フィリップが！」ラウルは大声をあげた。「捜してきます！」

彼は跳び上がり、戸口から走り出た。頭の中をさまざまな思いが駆けめぐり、またもや考えが混乱してきた。だが廊下を走りだしたとたん、不思議な男に呼び止められた。黒い肌に、輝く緑色の目。ラウルは前にこの男をオペラ座で見かけたことがあった。いったい誰だっただろう……そうだ、ペルシャ人だ！

「シャニー子爵」と、ペルシャ人が言った。「私はエリックという名の怪物を知っています。きっと彼がクリスティーヌを連れ去ったのです。私なら、彼女を救うお手伝いができるでしょう」

11. Down into the Cellars

"I know Erik well," said the Persian. "I feel partly responsible for what he has done. I feel that I should have let him die when I had the chance! Then he would never have caused so much trouble, death, and pain! But we don't have much time. You must follow me and do everything I say. Our lives depend on it."

Raoul studied the Persian. He was a tall man in dress clothes, and he wore a Persian hat. He looked like he was telling the truth. Besides, this was the only other person who knew about Erik! Raoul decided to follow him, and they hurried down the hall. They came to Christine's dressing room.

"In here," said the Persian. When they entered, the Persian knocked softly three times on the wall. Suddenly, a hidden door in the wall opened, and a short man also wearing a Persian hat entered. He put two guns on the table.

■would never have done 決して〜しなかったでしょう ■Persian hat ペルシャ帽
■hidden 形 隠された

11. 地下室へ

「私はエリックをよく知っているのです」とペルシャ人。「彼のしたことに、いくらか責任さえ感じています。機会があった時に殺しておくべきでした！ そうすれば、これほど多くの事件や殺人や傷害を起こすことはなかったのに！ ですが、もう時間がありません。私の後について、すべて言うとおりにしてください。我々の命はそれに掛かっています」

ラウルはペルシャ人をしげしげと見つめた。彼は背が高く、正装をしてペルシャ帽をかぶっていた。うそをついているようには見えなかった。そのうえ、他にエリックを知っているただ1人の人物なのだ！ ラウルは彼についていく決心をし、2人は急いで廊下を走った。そしてクリスティーヌの楽屋にやってきた。

「この中です」とペルシャ人。中に入ると、ペルシャ人は壁を3回、そっとノックした。するといきなり壁の隠し戸が開いて、やはりペルシャ帽をかぶった背の低い男が部屋に入ってきた。そして2丁のピストルをテーブルの上に置いた。

"This is my servant, Darius," the Persian explained to Raoul. "He knows the opera as well as I do. I sent for him and these guns as soon as I heard Christine went missing." The Persian turned to the man.

"Were you followed?" he asked. The man shook his head no.

"Thank you, Darius. You may go."

Darius left through the same hidden door. Raoul watched all this with surprise.

As the Persian checked the guns, he explained, "That door is one of the ways Erik gets into Christine's room. The other way is this."

He reached up to a corner of the wall near the ceiling. He pushed something there, and suddenly, the mirror doubled and opened up!

"Erik built all these things. Back in my country, Erik was called 'the trap-door lover.' Here, in Paris, he was one of the chief builders of this opera house."

All this information was creating more questions in Raoul's mind than answers. But there was no time for talking.

■send for ～を呼びにやる、取り寄せる ■follow 動 ～を尾行する ■reach up 背伸びをする ■open up 開く ■back in ～の当時 ■no time for doing ～している場合ではない

「召し使いのダリウスです」と、ペルシャ人がラウルに説明した。「私と同じくらいオペラ座のことをよく知っています。クリスティーヌが失踪したと聞いてすぐに、銃を持ってこさせたのです」。ペルシャ人は召使いの方に振り向いた。

「つけられなかったか？」と尋ねた。召使いは首を横に振った。

「ありがとう、ダリウス。もう行っていいぞ」

ダリウスは先ほどの隠し戸から出ていった。ラウルはすべてを驚きの目で見つめていた。

ペルシャ人は銃を確かめながら、説明した。「そのドアは、エリックがクリスティーヌの部屋に入るために使った道の1つです。そしてもう1つは、これですよ」

彼は天井近くの壁の隅に手を伸ばした。そのどこかを押すと、突然、鏡が二つ折りになって開いたのだ！

「エリックがこれを全部こしらえたのです。私の国で、エリックは『隠し戸愛好家』と呼ばれていました。ここパリでは、このオペラ座の建築主任の1人だったのです」

この情報を聞いて、ラウルの頭には答えよりも、むしろ多くの疑問が生じてきた。だが、話をしている時間はなかった。

"Here, take this gun. Be very quiet, and follow me!" said the Persian.

With that, the two men stepped through the mirror into a cold, dark hall.

"Before we go," said the Persian, "you must hold your gun out in front of you, as if you are about to shoot. Hold your whole arm out, and keep your hand at the same height as your eyes. Always hold your arm out like this! Now, let's go!"

Holding his gun in front of him, the Persian led the way deeper into the darkness.

They made their way through the cellars for what seemed to be a long time. Raoul was surprised at how well the Persian knew the opera house. The Persian was, perhaps, the best guide he could have asked for.

Most of the time they were able to walk, but sometimes they had to crawl through small spaces. No matter what, they always held their arms out as if they were about to shoot. When Raoul said that his arm was getting tired holding the gun this way, the Persian told him to put the gun in his pocket but to keep his arm out in front of him.

"But how could that possibly help?" asked Raoul.

■step through ～に足を踏み入れる　■hold something out （物）を差し出す　■lead the way 案内する　■ask for ～を依頼する　■crawl 這はって進む　■no matter what 何であろうとも

「さあ、銃を取りなさい。音を立てずに、私についてくるのですよ！」とペルシャ人。

そうして、2人の男は鏡を通りぬけ、冷たく暗い廊下に入った。

「出発する前に」とペルシャ人。「銃を前に構えなくてはいけません。今にも撃とうとするようにです。腕をいっぱいに伸ばして、手を目の高さに上げておきなさい。いつでも腕をこのように突き出しておくのですよ！　さあ、行きましょう！」

銃を前に構えながら、ペルシャ人は暗闇の中へ深く進んでいった。

いくつかの地下室を通り抜け、ずいぶん時間が経ったように思えた。ペルシャ人がオペラ座のことをあまりにもよく知っているので、ラウルは驚いた。おそらく、このペルシャ人ほどの案内人を頼むことはできなかっただろう。

ほとんどは歩くことができたが、狭い所をはって通らねばならない時もあった。それにもかかわらず、いつでもすぐ撃てるように銃を構えていた。ラウルが、こうして銃を持つのに腕が疲れてきたと言うと、ペルシャ人が、銃はポケットに入れてもいいが、腕は前に突き出しておくようにと答えた。

「でも、いったいそれがなんの役に立つんです？」と、ラウルが尋ねた。

The Persian turned around to face him. He was very serious.

  "I don't have enough time to explain everything," he said, "but I will tell you this much: Erik lived for some time in India. While he was there, he became very skilled at using rope. In fact, he became a master strangler. For a while, he earned money by fighting soldiers and strong men with only a rope. Just when the soldier, armed with a sword, thought he would win, Erik would throw the rope perfectly around the soldier's neck and pull the rope tight until he died. This is why you must hold your arm out. Erik could be looking for us, waiting for us, or following us. He won't be able to throw the rope around your neck if you're in this position. It is a matter of life or death."

  The Persian then continued on his way. Raoul followed without asking any more questions.

■strangler 图 絞殺魔　■armed with 〜で武装して　■continue on one's way そのまま歩き続ける

ペルシャ人が振り向いて、ラウルと顔を合わせた。とても真剣な顔つきだった。
「すべてを説明する時間はありません。でも、これだけは言っておきましょう。エリックはしばらくインドに住んでいました。その間に縄使いの技を習得したのです。それどころか絞殺の名手になり、しばらくの間、兵士や猛者と縄だけで戦って稼いでいました。剣を帯びた兵士が、勝てると思って油断していると、エリックが兵士の首に寸分違わず縄を投げ、息が絶えるまで締めつけたものです。ですから腕を突き出しておくのです。エリックは我々を捜しているか、待ち受けているか、もしくは後をつけているかもしれない。でもこの姿勢なら、首のまわりに縄を投げられないでしょう。生死を分けることですよ」

　それからペルシャ人は前進を続けた。ラウルはもう何も聞かずに、彼の後についていった。

12. Inside the Torture Room

Finally, they arrived in the third cellar, where Joseph Buquet was found hanging. The Persian knew this area was the back entrance to Erik's house because he had started to follow Erik several weeks ago. Once the Persian knew Erik was in love with Christine, he began to worry for her safety. He secretly followed Erik around to understand where he went, how he entered his house, and where he might end up taking Christine. One day, the Persian had followed Erik to this spot, where he had seen him remove a large stone from a wall. Erik had climbed into his house through the hole in the wall, and the Persian knew this was where they could enter.

"This is the back of Erik's house," whispered the Persian. "I believe it's safer to enter through here than the front, by the lake. Once we enter, we must not talk at all, for Erik might hear us."

■back entrance 裏口 ■be in love with 〜に恋して ■end up doing 最終的に〜することになる

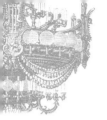

12. 拷問部屋の中

　ついに2人は、地下3階の部屋にたどり着いた。ジョゼフ・ビュケが首をつって発見されたところだ。ペルシャ人は、この場所がエリックの家の裏口だと知っていた。数週間前からエリックの後をつけていたからだ。エリックがクリスティーヌに恋をしていると知って、ペルシャ人は彼女の身が心配になった。そこで密かにエリックの後をつけ、どこへ行き、どうやって家に入り、最後はどこへクリスティーヌを連れ去るつもりか調べようとした。ある日、ペルシャ人はエリックの後をつけてこの場所までやってきた。そしてエリックが壁から大きな石をどけるのを目にした。エリックは壁に開いた穴を通って家にもぐりこんだ。それで、ここから家に入れるとわかったのだ。

「これがエリックの家の裏側です」と、ペルシャ人はささやいた。「湖畔にある玄関より、こちらから入る方がきっと安全でしょう。中に入ったら、決して声を出してはいけませんよ。エリックに聞こえるかもしれませんから」

The Persian reached up and carefully removed a large stone from the wall.

"Take off your shoes," he mouthed to Raoul. Then, he climbed up and in through the hole, disappearing into Erik's house. Raoul followed.

When Raoul quietly dropped to the ground, he saw something that shocked him. Although it was quite dark, he could see that they were in a forest. Many men were there with them! The Persian saw Raoul's eyes open wide with surprise, and he took hold of the young man's arm. The Persian walked towards one of the trees and put Raoul's hand on it. It was cold—how strange! It was made of iron. Then the Persian walked towards one of the men, who also started walking toward him! The Persian put his hand out, and the man also put his hand out. Their hands touched. Raoul finally realized what was happening. It was a mirror! All the walls were mirrors!

Looking carefully, Raoul could see that there was only one iron tree in the room, and they were the only men. He could also see the edges of the mirrors where they met. He counted six mirrors. So they had dropped into a small, six-sided room made entirely of mirrors. What kind of place was this?

■mouth 動声を出さずに口の形だけで言う ■iron 名鉄 ■put one's hand out 手を差し出す ■six-sided 形六面の

ペルシャ人は腕を伸ばし、壁から大きな石を慎重にどけた。

　「靴を脱いで」と、口だけ動かしてラウルに伝えた。それからよじ登って穴の中にもぐりこみ、エリックの家へと消えていった。ラウルも後に続いた。

　そっと地面に下りた時、ラウルは驚くべきものを目にした。やはり真っ暗だが、どうやら森の中らしい。しかも大勢の男たちが一緒にいるのだ！ペルシャ人は、ラウルが驚きで目をみはっているのに気づいて、彼の腕をつかんだ。そして１本の木に近づくと、それにラウルの手を触れさせた。冷たい——変だぞ！　これは鉄製だ。それからペルシャ人が１人の男に近づくと、その男もこちらへ向かってくるではないか！　ペルシャ人が手を前に差しだすと、その男も手を差しだした。そして２人の手が触れあった。ラウルはやっと何が起こっているのか気がついた。鏡だ！　壁がすべて鏡になっているのだ！

　よく見てみると、部屋には鉄の木が１本あるだけで、人間も自分たちしかいないことがわかった。鏡の合わせ目も見えた。数えると、鏡は６枚あった。ということは、２人は６面の鏡だけでできた小部屋に落ち込んだのだ。これはいったいどういう場所なのだろう？

12. 拷問部屋の中

The Persian looked all around him and knew that they had entered a terrible place. In Persia, he had seen Erik build a room like this for the king. It was a torture room. The Persian looked at the iron tree and saw something that filled him with fear. A rope hung from a branch. The Persian thought of Joseph Buquet. Perhaps this was the rope from which he had hung.

Suddenly, the two men heard footsteps in a room nearby. Then they heard a voice.

"I love you, Christine. But you do not love me!"

It was Erik! Then, they heard Christine crying. She was alive!

"I will give you a choice," said Erik. "You have until eleven o'clock tomorrow to decide: Will we play the wedding song or the song for the dead? The wedding song is very lovely, Christine. The song for the dead is not quite as nice. You must decide either to marry me or die with me!"

Christine said nothing, though she continued to cry.

■torture 图拷問　■branch 图枝　■not quite as さほど〜ではない

ペルシャ人はまわりを見まわして、恐ろしい場所に入ってしまったことに気づいた。ペルシャで、エリックが王のためにこのような部屋を作っているのを見たことがある。拷問部屋だ。鉄の木を見ると、あるものが目に入って恐怖に襲われた。枝からロープがぶら下がっている。ジョゼフ・ビュケのことを思い出した。おそらく彼が首をつったロープだろう。

　突然、2人は近くの部屋で足音がするのを耳にした。それから声が聞こえた。
　「愛しているよ、クリスティーヌ。だが君は私を愛していない！」
　エリックだ！　すると、クリスティーヌの泣く声が聞こえた。彼女は生きている！
　「君にチャンスをあげよう」とエリック。「明日の11時までに決めるがいい。結婚の歌を奏でるか、もしくは死の歌にするかね？　結婚の歌はじつに美しいよ、クリスティーヌ。死の歌はそれほど良くはない。私と結婚するか、一緒に死ぬか決めるのだ！」

　クリスティーヌは何も答えず、ただ泣き続けた。

"I know what will help you decide, my love. If you do not choose to marry me, we will not be the only ones to die. *Everyone* will die! I have a plan, you see. If we do not marry at eleven o'clock tomorrow night, everyone will be dead!"

The Persian became very concerned. What did Erik mean? How would everyone die? What was his plan?

Just then, there was a loud ringing sound, like an alarm clock.

"A visitor at the lake!" cried Erik angrily. "Who could have come down here? I must go tell this visitor he is not wanted!" He rushed across the room and they all heard a door open and close behind him.

This was Raoul's chance. He called out, "Christine! Christine! It is Raoul! We will save you!"

Christine called back, "Raoul? Can it really be you? Oh, you must run! Run far away from this place!"

"Christine," the Persian cut in, "I am here to help Raoul. But we are trapped in a room with no door. All the walls in here are mirrors. I believe it is the torture room. Can you get us out of here?"

■concerned 形 心配して　■ringing 形 鳴り響く　■call back 呼び返す　■cut in 割り込む　■be trapped in ～に閉じ込められる

「どうすれば決められるかはわかっているよ、愛しいクリスティーヌ。私との結婚を選ばなければ、死ぬのは我々だけではない。皆が死ぬのだ！　いい計画があるのだよ。もし明日の夜11時に結婚しなければ、全員死ぬことになるのだ！」

ペルシャ人はひどく不安になってきた。エリックはどうするつもりだろう？　どうやって皆を殺そうというのか？　彼の計画とは？

ちょうどそのとき、目覚まし時計のような、大きなベルの音がした。

「湖に誰か来たな！」エリックが腹立たしげに怒鳴った。「ここまで来るとは、いったい何者だ？　この訪問者に、じゃまをするなと言いに行かねばならん！」彼は部屋を走っていき、ドアの開く音と閉まる音がした。

これはラウルにとってチャンスだった。彼は大声で呼びかけた。「クリスティーヌ！　クリスティーヌ！　ラウルだよ！　助けてあげるからね！」

クリスティーヌが呼び返した。「ラウル？　本当にあなたなの？　まあ、逃げなきゃだめよ！　ここから遠くへ逃げてちょうだい！」

「クリスティーヌ」ペルシャ人が割りこんだ。「手助けの者です。でも出口のない部屋に閉じ込められました。どの壁も鏡だから、きっと拷問部屋でしょう。出してもらえますか？」

"I can't!" cried out Christine. "I'm tied up!"

"That monster!" said Raoul. "Why has he tied you?"

"I tried to kill myself. When he brought me down here, I tried to kill myself by hitting my head against the wall. He tied me up, for I am not allowed to die until eleven o'clock tomorrow."

"No!" cried Raoul.

"Never mind," said the Persian. He knew they had to act quickly. He called out to Christine, "Listen to me, my dear. Do you know where the door to the torture room is?"

"No," she replied. "But I know where he keeps the keys!"

"Good! Now listen closely. Erik loves you. Because of this, you have power over him. Be sweet to him and tell him what he wants to hear. Then have him untie you. If you are free to move, my dear, you can get the key, and we will figure out how to get out of here safely!"

Suddenly, they heard the monster enter again.

"I'm back, my love," he said to Christine. "I'm sorry I had to go, but we don't want any visitors, do we? Don't worry, I took care of him. He won't ever visit again."

■tie up 縛り上げる　■kill oneself 自殺する　■allow to do 〜することを許す　■never mind 大丈夫、心配しないで　■listen closely しっかり耳をかたむける　■be sweet to 〜にやさしい　■untie 動（結び目などを）解く　■figure out（解決法などを）見つけ出す　■take care of 〜を始末する

「できないわ！」と、クリスティーヌが叫んだ。「縛られているのよ！」
「あの怪物め！」とラウル。「どうして縛ったりするんだ？」
「私、自殺しようとしたの。ここに連れてこられた時、頭を壁に打ちつけて死のうとしたのよ。そしたら、あの人に縛られたの。明日の11時までは死なさないって」

「なんてことだ！」と、ラウルは叫んだ。
「大丈夫ですよ」とペルシャ人。早く行動しなければいけないとわかっていたからだ。クリスティーヌに呼びかけた。「聞いてください。拷問部屋の入口はわかりますか？」
「いいえ」彼女は答えた。「でも、鍵のある所は知っています！」
「よかった！　さあ、よく聞いて。エリックはあなたを愛しています。ですから、あなたには彼を操る力があるのです。エリックにやさしくして、聞きたがるようなことを言ってやりなさい。そうして縄を解かせるのです。解かれて動けるようになったら、鍵を取れるし、無事に脱出する方法も見つかるでしょう！」
そのとたん、怪物がまた入ってくる音がした。
「ただいま、愛しいクリスティーヌ」と、エリックは言った。「留守にしてすまなかった。だが訪問者など不要だろう？　心配いらないよ、私が始末した。もう二度と来ないよ」

Both Raoul and the Persian wondered who the poor visitor was. Who would know to come down here, to the house by the lake? Whoever he was, what had happened to him?

Then Christine spoke softly.

"No, I don't care for visitors when you are with me, Erik."

Yes, thought the Persian. That's right, Christine! Be sweet and use your power over him!

"Erik, dear, can you please untie me? These ropes are hurting me."

"Oh, my love! Have I hurt you? I am so sorry ... Is that better?"

"Yes, much better. Thank you."

"I know what will make you feel better, my love. Music! You shall hear me play the song for the dead for our little visitor!"

Raoul and the Persian's hearts turned cold. So the visitor must be dead! They heard Erik run into another room and begin to play the organ. He played beautifully. But suddenly he stopped and cried out, "Where is my bag with the keys?"

There were loud footsteps, and soon the two men heard Christine cry out in pain.

■poor 気の毒な　■care for ～に関心を持つ　■Can you please ~? どうか～してもらえませんか？　■turn cold 冷え切る

ラウルもペルシャ人も、その哀れな訪問者は誰だろうと思った。いったい誰がこの湖畔の家への道を知っているのだろう？　また誰であろうと、その人に何があったのか？
　すると、クリスティーヌがやさしく話しかけた。
「いいえ、誰が来ようと、あなたが一緒にいてくれれば平気よ、エリック」
　いいぞ、とペルシャ人は思った。その調子だ、クリスティーヌ！　やさしくして彼を操れ！
「エリック、ねえ、縄をほどいてくれない？　この縄、とても痛いのよ」

「ああ、愛しいクリスティーヌ！　痛かったかい？　許しておくれ……これでどうだい？」
「ええ、とてもよくなったわ。ありがとう」
「どうすればもっと気分がよくなるか知っているよ。音楽だ！　哀れな訪問者の死を悼む曲を弾いてあげるから聞いてごらん！」

　ラウルとペルシャ人の心が凍りついた。それでは、訪問者は死んだに違いない！　エリックが別の部屋へ走っていき、オルガンを弾きだすのが聞こえた。素晴らしい演奏だった。ところが突然、彼は手を止めて叫んだ。「鍵を入れた袋はどこだ？」
　大きな足音がしたと思うと、直後にクリスティーヌの痛がる悲鳴が聞こえた。

She must have taken the keys, thought the Persian, and he must have hurt her to get them back.

"Aha!" cried Erik. "Why are you stealing from me? You mustn't ever steal from Erik!"

Again, Christine cried out in pain.

Raoul, unable to control himself, cried out, "Leave her alone!"

"What?" said Erik. "There is someone here! Christine, you know there is someone here and you are trying to help him! You are trying to run away! Well, I won't let you! And I shall teach your friend a lesson he won't forget!"

They heard Erik's footsteps come toward the torture room. It sounded like he was climbing some stairs, and then they heard the sound of a curtain being pushed aside. A little light suddenly came into the torture room. Raoul and the Persian looked up, and there, near the ceiling, was a narrow window, just big enough for a pair of eyes to look through. They saw two eyes like black holes, angry eyes, looking down at them.

■get something back（物）を取り戻す　■aha 間ははあ、なるほど　■steal 動盗む
■push aside 横にずらす　■look through ～をのぞく

彼女が鍵を取ったに違いない、とペルシャ人は思った。そしてきっとエリックが痛い目にあわせて取り返そうとしているのだ。

「ほう、そういうことか！」エリックが叫んだ。「なぜ盗もうとする？　このエリックから盗むなど決して許さんぞ！」

再び、クリスティーヌが痛そうに悲鳴をあげた。

ラウルは自分を抑えられなくなり、思わず怒鳴った。「クリスティーヌを離せ！」

「なんだと？」とエリック。「ここに誰かいるな！　クリスティーヌ、誰かいるのを知って、助けようとしているのか！　逃げるつもりだな！　なるほど、だが、そうはさせんぞ！　それから君の友人にも忘れがたい教訓を教えてやろう！」

エリックの足音が拷問部屋に近づいてきた。階段を上がるような足音がし、カーテンを開ける音が聞こえた。そのとたん、小さな光が拷問部屋に差し込んだ。ラウルとペルシャ人が見上げると、天井の近くに、ちょうど両目でのぞけるくらいの狭い窓があった。黒い穴のような２つの目が、怒りに燃えて２人を見下ろしている。

"Your friends are hiding in the torture room," said Erik. "Well, let's give them a *warm* welcome. I believe they will be feeling quite warm soon!"

Suddenly, very bright, very hot lights turned on in the torture room. Raoul and the Persian started to sweat.

"These lights!" cried Raoul. "They are so bright and hot—it feels like we will burn alive!"

"Raoul, we must stay calm," said the Persian. "The heat will make us lose our minds if we are not careful. This is how Erik tortures people. Once you decide you cannot take any more heat, it is very easy to tell yourself to use the rope on that tree! You must stay calm. I know Erik well, so I will look for the hidden button that will open the door to let us out of here."

Raoul was silent. The Persian got to work looking for the hidden button. He felt and studied every inch of each mirror carefully. He was done with three, with only three left to go, when Raoul began to talk of water.

"I must drink ... I don't know how much longer I can take this ... "

■sweat 動 汗をかく ■burn 動 燃える ■lose one's mind 正気を失う ■look for 〜を探す ■every inch of 〜のすみずみまで

「君の友人たちが拷問部屋に隠れているよ」とエリック。「よし、暖かく歓迎してやるとしよう。きっとすぐ、まさに暖かくなるだろうよ！」

 すると突然、ひどくまぶしくて熱い光が、拷問部屋の中を照らした。ラウルとペルシャ人は汗ばみはじめた。

「この光！」ラウルが叫んだ。「とてもまぶしくて熱いぞ──生きたまま焼かれそうだ！」

「ラウル、落ち着くのです」とペルシャ人。「気をつけないと、暑さで正気を失いますよ。エリックはこうして人々を拷問するのです。もう暑さに耐えられないと思ったとたん、あの木にかかったロープで首をつりたくなりますよ。落ち着きなさい。私はエリックをよく知っています。ですから、出口のドアを開ける隠しボタンを探しましょう」

 ラウルは黙った。ペルシャ人は隠しボタンを探し始めた。それぞれの鏡をすみずみまで慎重に触りながら調べた。3枚調べ終わり、残りあと3枚という時に、ラウルが水を欲しがりだした。

「水をくれ……もうあとどれくらい耐えられるかわからない……」

"Raoul!" said the Persian, going to him, "You must stay strong! Do not think of water. Don't worry, I will find the button soon."

But when the Persian turned back to the mirrors, he wasn't sure which he had already studied and which were left. He had to begin all over again!

Neither of them knew how much time had passed. Raoul lay on the ground. He couldn't speak in full sentences.

"Christine ... The monster won't let us out ... Water ... "

By this time, the Persian was not doing much better. He could not see straight, and his legs gave out. He fell to the floor. Under the bright lights, both men closed their eyes and slipped into darkness.

■all over again 最初からやり直して　■lie on the ground 地面に横たわる　■give out へたばる　■slip into いつしか〜の状態になる

「ラウル！」ペルシャ人はそう言って、ラウルに近寄った。「しっかりするのです！　水のことを考えてはいけません。心配しないで、すぐにボタンを見つけますから」

ところが、ペルシャ人が鏡のところに戻ると、どの鏡を調べ終わり、どれがまだなのかわからなくなっていた。また最初からやり直さなければならなかったのだ！

どれほど時間が経ったのか、2人ともわからなかった。ラウルは床に横になっている。もうまともに話すこともできなかった。

「クリスティーヌ……怪物から逃げられそうにない……水を……」

このころには、ペルシャ人の仕事もあまりはかどらなくなっていた。目がかすみ、足も立たない。ついに床に倒れた。まぶしい光の下で、2人とも目を閉じて暗闇の中へ落ちていった。

13. The Scorpion and the Grasshopper

The Persian did not know how long he had been lying there when he awoke. As his vision came back to him, he saw a small black nail sticking out of the floor near the iron tree.

His eyes opened wide and he quickly sat up.

"Raoul! Wake up! I've found it!"

He knew this had to be the button to the door.

Raoul sat up with some difficulty. The Persian reached out and pressed the button.

A trap-door in the floor opened down into a dark staircase.

"Come, Raoul!"

They went down into the dark, feeling the cool air on their hot faces. They smiled like children and continued to go down. Soon they came to a room full of barrels.

"Perhaps it's water! Or wine!" cried Raoul.

Both men quickly took a barrel and opened it. But what they found was not water or wine—it was gun powder!

■vision 名視力　■nail 名くぎ　■stick out of 〜から突き出る　■barrel 名樽
■gun powder 火薬

13. サソリとバッタ

　気がついた時、ペルシャ人はどれくらいそこに倒れていたのかわからなかった。視界がはっきりしてくると、鉄の木のそばの床から、小さな黒いくぎが突き出ているのが見えた。
　目を大きく見開いて、彼はすばやく起き直った。
「ラウル！　起きなさい！　見つけましたよ！」
　これがドアを開けるボタンに違いないと、彼にはわかっていた。
　ラウルがやっとのことで起き上がった。ペルシャ人は手を伸ばしてボタンを押した。
　床の隠し戸が下に開き、暗い階段が見えた。
「来なさい、ラウル！」
　彼らが暗闇のなかへ下りていくと、火照った顔に冷たい空気が触れるのを感じた。2人は子どものように顔をほころばせ、下りつづけた。やがて、樽でいっぱいの部屋に着いた。
「たぶん水だ！　それかワインだ！」ラウルが声を張りあげた。
　2人はすばやく樽を取り、ふたを開けた。ところが、中に入っていたのは水でもワインでもなかった——火薬だ！

The Persian went cold with fear. He now knew Erik's plan. If Christine didn't marry him, he was going to blow up the Paris Opera House! The arranged time of eleven o'clock now made sense to him: it was the time the opera was filled with people watching a show.

"What time is it?" cried the Persian. "How long have we been here? It may be too late!"

They ran up the steps to the torture room, but the light was now turned off. Erik must have realized they had escaped. Suddenly, they heard Christine's voice.

"Raoul! Raoul!"

"Christine! Are you safe? There's gun powder here, Christine! He means to blow up the whole opera house! We must stop him, Christine! What time is it?"

"It is five minutes to eleven!" she replied. "I must marry him, Raoul. Forgive me! I must marry him or everyone will die! He has left to prepare some final things. He said there are two boxes here on the table. One holds a scorpion and the other a grasshopper. They are both made of iron. If I choose to marry him, I'm to turn the scorpion. If I choose death, I'm to turn the grasshopper."

■go cold 冷え冷えとする ■blow up 爆破する ■arranged 形用意された ■make sense 意味が通る ■turn off（スイッチなどを）切る ■five minutes to 〜の五分前 ■scorpion 图サソリ ■grasshopper 图バッタ

13. The Scorpion and the Grasshopper

ペルシャ人は恐怖で凍りついた。エリックの計画がわかったのだ。もしクリスティーヌがエリックと結婚しなかったら、パリ・オペラ座を爆破するつもりだ！　時刻を11時に決めた理由もわかった。それは、オペラ座が芝居の観客で満員になる時刻だ。

　「今何時だ？」ペルシャ人は叫んだ。「何時間ここにいた？　もう手遅れかもしれない！」
　彼らは階段を駆け上がって拷問部屋へ戻ったが、すでに光が消えていた。エリックが２人の脱出に気づいたに違いない。するとそのとき、クリスティーヌの声が聞こえた。
　「ラウル！　ラウル！」
　「クリスティーヌ！　無事かい？　ここに火薬があるんだ、クリスティーヌ！　エリックはオペラ座ごと爆破するつもりだ！　止めなくては、クリスティーヌ！　今何時だ？」
　「あと５分で11時よ！」彼女は答えた。「私、あの人と結婚しなきゃ、ラウル。許してね！　結婚しないと、みんなが死ぬのよ！　あの人は最後の準備をしに行ったわ。テーブルの上に２つの箱があるそうよ。１つにはサソリ、もう１つにはバッタが入っていて、どちらも鉄でできているの。結婚を選ぶならサソリを回すのよ。死を選ぶならバッタですって」

"Wait!" cried the Persian. "You say they are made of iron and you must turn one?"

"Yes!"

"Don't touch either!" cried the Persian. "They are both devices! I'm sure the grasshopper is connected to something that will blow up the gun powder. I believe the scorpion is connected to something too, I just don't know what!"

Just then they all heard Erik's voice. He had returned, and he had heard them talking.

"Very good, my friend!" he said. "You are correct! But it is Christine's choice, and it is now eleven o'clock. You must choose, Christine. To marry me, turn the scorpion! To die, turn the grasshopper!"

Raoul and the Persian held their breath as they waited. Suddenly, they heard a sound—but it wasn't an explosion, it was the sound of water!

"Christine chooses the scorpion!" Erik cried. "Come! We must be married!"

"But what will happen with the scorpion?" cried out Christine.

■device 名 装置　■just then その途端に　■hold one's breath 息をのむ

「待ちなさい！」ペルシャ人が叫んだ。「どちらも鉄製で、一方を回すのですね？」

「そうよ！」

「どちらも触ってはいけません！」ペルシャ人が声を張りあげた。「両方とも装置です！　きっと、バッタは火薬を爆発させるものに接続されているのです。サソリも何かにつながれているのでしょう、何かはわかりませんが！」

ちょうどそのとき、エリックの声が皆に聞こえた。彼は戻ってきて話を聞いていたのだ。

「上出来だ、わが友よ！」とエリック。「そのとおりだよ！　だが選ぶのはクリスティーヌだ。そして、今は11時。さあ、選ばなければならないよ、クリスティーヌ。私と結婚するなら、サソリを回しなさい！　死ぬなら、バッタを回すのだ！」

ラウルとペルシャ人は息をつめて待った。突然、音が聞こえた——だが爆発音ではない。水の音だ！

「クリスティーヌはサソリを選んだぞ！」エリックが叫んだ。「おいで！結婚するのだ！」

「だけど、サソリを回したら何が起こるの？」クリスティーヌが叫んだ。

"Turning it releases water from the lake to flow into the room holding the gun powder. All the powder will be washed away. You have saved everyone at the opera, my love. However, you must say goodbye to Raoul and his friend, for the water will fill the torture room too! Now, come!"

As Erik spoke, the water rushed into the lower room with the barrels, and it quickly came up the stairs. Raoul and the Persian tried wildly to find some way out. The water rose quickly, coming up to their knees.

They cried out for help, but there was no answer.

"Erik! Erik!" cried the Persian. "I saved your life once! In Persia, you were sentenced to death and I set you free! How can you repay me like this?"

There was no answer. Erik had taken Christine away and now the two men were alone to face their deaths.

The water was now up to their necks. They swam around, hitting and kicking at the mirrored walls. As the water neared the ceiling, they took their last breaths ...

■flow into 〜に流れ込む　■wash away 洗い流す　■be sentenced to death 死刑宣告を受ける　■set someone free（人）を解放する　■repay 動 恩に報いる　■face 動 〜に直面する

「それを回すと、湖の水が放たれて火薬の部屋へ流れ込むのだ。火薬はすべて洗い流されるだろう。君はオペラ座の人々を全員救ったのだよ。だが、ラウルとその友人にはお別れを言わねばならん。拷問部屋も水で満たされるからね！　さあ、おいで！」

　エリックが話している間にも、樽のある下の部屋に水がなだれ込み、あっという間に階段を上がってきた。ラウルとペルシャ人は、必死に出口を探そうとした。水はどんどん上がってきて、ひざの高さまでになった。

　2人は助けを求めて叫んだが、返事はなかった。
「エリック！　エリック！」ペルシャ人が叫んだ。「私は一度おまえの命を救った！　ペルシャで死刑を宣告された時、逃がしてやっただろう！　よくもこんな形で返せるものだな！」
　それでも返事はなかった。エリックはクリスティーヌを連れ去り、今や2人は死を前にして置き去りにされたのだ。
　水はもう首まで上がってきていた。彼らは鏡の壁を叩いたり、けったりして泳ぎまわった。水が天井に近づいた時、2人は最後の息を吸った……。

覚えておきたい英語表現［文法］

疑問詞それとも関係副詞？

基本文法をおさらいすると、読みが確実になります。物語を楽しみながら、合わせて文法力もつけましょう。ここでは、同じ疑問詞に見えても様々な働きがあることを復習しましょう。意味深なitの使い方も説明します。

> <u>No matter what</u>, they always held their arms out <u>as if</u> they <u>were</u> about to shoot. (p.134, 下から6行目)
> 何がどうであれ、いつでもすぐ撃てるように銃を構えていた。

【解説】まずは後半の節。as if は「あたかも〜するかのように」。「be (just) about to不定詞」で「まさに〜しようとしている」と、be going to より差し迫った未来を表します。後半を直訳すれば、「彼らはまさに撃とうとしているかのように常に腕を突き出していた」、つまり「いつでも撃てるように銃を構えていた」という意味になります。文頭の No matter what, は「何があっても」「何がどうあれ」と譲歩を表します。what の次に happened が省略されたかたちです。happens/happened の代わりに他の動詞や主語+動詞をつなげることができます。

【例文】　I will believe you, <u>no matter what</u> (happens).
　　　　どんなことがあってもあなたを信じます。

　　　　<u>No matter what</u>, I have nothing to lose.
　　　　何がどうあれ、失うものはない。

　　　　<u>No matter what</u> you say, I can't trust you.
　　　　あなたが何を言っても、信用できない。

　no matter whatと同じように、「no matter + 疑問詞」で複合関係詞と同じく、「〜しても」と譲歩を表すことができます。例えば、
　　no matter how = however（どんなふうに〜しても）
　　no matter when = whenever（いつ〜しようとも）
　　no matter where = wherever（どこで〜しようとも）　等々

> He secretly followed Erik around to understand where he went, how he entered his house, and where he might end up taking Christine.（p.138, 5行目）
> 彼は密かにエリックの後をつけ、どこへ行き、どうやって家に入り、最後はどこへクリスティーヌを連れ去るつもりか調べようとした。

【解説】where 以下は間接疑問文で、understand の目的語になっています。疑問文が文の一部分になったものを間接疑問文と言いますが、普通の疑問文の語順とは違って、疑問詞の次は平叙文のかたちになります。where や how だけでなく、what, when など、他の疑問詞でも同じように間接疑問文を作ることができます。

【例文】　I wonder where my cellphone went.
　　　　　私の携帯どこに行ったのかしら。

　　　　　When this statue was made is not known.
　　　　　この像がいつ作られたのかわかっていない。

> One day, the Persian had followed Erik to this spot, where he had seen him remove a large stone from a wall.（p.138, 8行目）
> ある日、ペルシャ人はエリックの後をつけてこの場所までやって来た。そしてエリックが壁から大きな石をどけるのを目にした。

【解説】この文のwhere は疑問詞ではなく、関係副詞です。関係副詞は、副詞の働きと二つの文を結びつける接続詞の両方の働きをします。前半の文のthis spot を受けて、「そしてその場所で」と次の文をつなげています。where の前にカンマ（,）がありますので、この関係副詞は、非制限用法（継続用法）。前の文を追加説明しているだけで、this spotがどのような場所なのかを限定しているわけではありません。

【例文】　Christine went to Perros, where her father was buried.
　　　　　クリスティーヌはペロスに行ったが、そこには彼女の父親が葬られていた。

　　　　　cf. It is at the bottom of the hill where we used to play as children.
　　　　　それは私たちがかつてこどものときに遊んだ丘のふもとにあります。

　　　　　＊この場合の where は、どんな丘か、the hill を限定しているので、制限［限定］用法と言います。

> Erik had climbed into his house through the hole in the wall, and he knew this was <u>where</u> they could enter. (p.138, 下から6行目)
> エリックは壁に開いた穴を通って家にもぐりこんだ。それで、ここから家に入れるとわかったのだ。

【解説】この文のwhereは関係副詞ですが、先行詞のthe placeが省略されています。and以下の文を直訳すれば、「彼はこれが中に入れるところだとわかった」となります。

　the time when, the reason why も 先行詞のthe timeやthe reasonがしばしば省略されます。when, whyが単独で使われ、「～するとき」「～する理由」という意味を表します。ただしhowは常に先行詞なしで使われ、the way howという言い方はありません。

【例文】　This is <u>where</u> they first met each other.
　　　　　ここで彼らは最初に出会いました。

　　　　　That is <u>where</u> you'll find a new world.
　　　　　そこには新たな世界がある。

　whereやwhenは、疑問詞のように見えても、関係副詞の働きをしていることがあって、ややこしいですね。文全体の構造がつかめれば、単語の働きも見えてきます。

　　　S（主語）＋V（動詞）＋O（目的語）＋〈どのように＋どこ＋いつ＋なぜ〉
　　　S（主語）＋V（動詞）＋C（補語）＋〈どのように＋どこ＋いつ＋なぜ〉

　ほとんどの文は、この2つの順番に並んでいますから、まずはこの文構造をつかむことが、読みの正確さにつながります。S, V, O, Cのポジションは順番が決まったレギュラー席、〈どのように＋どこ＋いつ＋なぜ〉は、副詞で動詞や文に説明を加えるおまけの部分です。これらが見分けられるかどうかが、読解のポイント。文の意味は文法で決まります。

> And she <u>meant</u> <u>it</u>! (p.176, 5行目)
> 彼女は本気だった！

【解説】mean itで「本気で言っている」「冗談で言っているのではない」という意味になります。会話でよく使われる便利な表現です。

【例文】　I <u>mean</u> <u>it</u> this time.　今度は本気で言っているのよ。

　　　　I didn't <u>mean</u> <u>it</u>.　そんなつもりじゃなかったんです。（わざとじゃないんです。）

　　　　Do you <u>mean</u> <u>it</u>?　本気なの？

> I did not know <u>if</u> you would <u>make</u> <u>it</u>. (p.176, 11行目)
> 君が助かるかどうかわからなかった。

【解説】ifは「もし」という意味ではなく、「〜かどうか」という意味の接続詞。if節が動詞knowの目的語になっています。make it のitは漠然と目標を指し、make itには「成功する」「うまくやる」「目的地にたどりつく」「間に合う」「回復する」「なんとか出席する」など、いろいろな意味があります。ここでは、「回復する」という意味で使われています。make itも会話でしょっちゅう出てくる表現で、とても便利ですが、意味が広いので文脈にそって意味を考える必要があります。

【例文】　If you try, you can <u>make</u> <u>it</u>.　なせばなる。

　　　　It looks like we are going to <u>make</u> <u>it</u>.　なんとか間に合いそうです。

　　　　Thank you for inviting me to your party. But I'm afraid I can't <u>make</u> <u>it</u>.
　　　　パーティーによんでくれてありがとう。でも行けそうにありません。

　I tried to make it as easy as possible for you to understand some grammar rules.
　文法をできるだけわかりやすく説明したつもりですが、"You made it!"と言っていただけたら光栄です。

Part 5

14. The End of the Ghost's Love

When the Persian woke up, he found himself in a bed. Christine and Erik were looking over him. Christine gently put her hand on his head. Then Erik helped him drink a glass of water.

"What happened?" asked the Persian after he had drunk.

"My wife saved your lives," said Erik. The Persian looked at Christine, but she said nothing. He looked around the room and saw Raoul sleeping on a sofa.

"Go back to sleep," said Erik. "When you are well enough, I will take you back to your homes. I do this to please my wife. She begged for your lives and I hate to see her in pain."

The Persian was still very weak and could not stay awake. He fell back asleep trying to understand what Erik was saying.

■find oneself 気がつくと〜している ■look over 〜を見下ろす ■please 動 〜を喜ばせる ■beg for someone's life（人）の命乞いをする

14. 怪人の恋の終わり

　気がつくと、ペルシャ人はベッドに寝かされていた。クリスティーヌとエリックが見下ろしている。クリスティーヌがやさしく彼の頭に手を当て、エリックが水を飲ませた。

　「どうなってるんだ？」ペルシャ人は水を飲んでから聞いた。
　「妻が君たちの命を救ったのだ」とエリック。ペルシャ人はクリスティーヌを見たが、彼女は何も言わなかった。部屋を見まわすと、ラウルがソファーで眠っていた。
　「もう一度眠るがいい」とエリック。「十分よくなったら家まで送って行こう。こうするのは妻を喜ばせるためだ。君たちの命を助けてくれと頼むし、妻が苦しむのは見たくないからね」
　ペルシャ人はまだとても弱っていたので、起きてはいられなかった。エリックの言葉の意味を考えようとするうちに、また眠りに落ちていった。

The next time the Persian awoke, he was in his own bed at home. Darius, his servant, was there, looking after him. When he asked what had happened to him, Darius said he had found him lying in the doorway of his house last night. He had been left there by a tall stranger who wore a mask.

It took a few days for the Persian to recover. As soon as he was well enough to walk, he went to the Count of Chagny's house to see if Raoul and Philippe were all right. But when he arrived, he found out that Raoul had disappeared, and Philippe was dead. The older Chagny brother had been found by the lake under the opera.

"The visitor at the lake!" thought the Persian. "Philippe must have been trying to find Raoul. He loved his younger brother so very dearly! But how had he known to come to the lake? Perhaps he had talked to the managers of the opera, who had heard Raoul's story about Erik and hadn't believed him … Perhaps Philippe had believed him … "

The Persian went back home with sadness in his heart. He could easily imagine what had happened to Philippe. He found his way to the lake, but once there, he must have set off the alarm. Erik went and found him … Then killed him with his rope … But the Persian couldn't imagine what could have happened to Raoul, or where he could be.

■look after 〜の世話をする　■doorway 图出入り口　■find one's way to 〜にたどり着く　■set off 作動させる

次に目を覚ました時には、自分の家のベッドの中にいた。召使いのダリウスが、そばで看病をしていた。何があったのか尋ねると、昨夜、家の入口で倒れているのを見つけたのだという。背が高く、仮面をつけた見知らぬ男が、彼を置いていったそうだ。

　ペルシャ人が回復するのには数日かかった。歩けるほどに治るとすぐに、ラウルとフィリップの無事を確かめようと、シャニー伯爵の家へ向かった。ところが着いてみると、ラウルは失踪し、フィリップは死んだことがわかった。シャニー兄弟の兄は、オペラ座の地下湖のそばで発見されたのだ。

「湖の訪問者だ！」ペルシャ人は思った。「フィリップはラウルを捜そうとしたに違いない。弟のことを心底かわいがっていたからな！　だが、湖への行き方をどうやって知ったのだろう？　おそらくオペラ座の支配人に聞いたのだろう。支配人たちはラウルからエリックのことを聞いたのに信じなかった……たぶんフィリップは信じたのだ……」

　ペルシャ人は胸に悲しみを抱えて家路についた。フィリップに何が起きたかは、容易に想像できる。彼は湖への道を見つけたが、着いたとたん、警報器を鳴らしてしまったに違いない。エリックが行って彼を見つけ……それから縄で絞殺し……。しかし、いったいラウルに何が起こり、今どこにいるのか、ペルシャ人にはまるでわからなかった。

14. 怪人の恋の終わり

The Persian reported all of this to the police, but he was laughed away. Everyone thought he was mad. Left without any other choice, he began to write down everything he knew. For days he wrote, and when he was almost finished, a visitor came to his house. Darius helped a very thin, tall man in a black cape and mask into the Persian's room. It was Erik!

He seemed very weak, and Darius had to help him walk. He sank into a chair and said quietly, "Hello, old friend."

"Murderer!" cried the Persian. "You killed Philippe de Chagny! Now, what have you done to Raoul and Christine?"

Erik put his hand over his heart and said, "They are together now, and they are free."

"What?"

"I came to tell you that I am dying. I am dying of love for Christine! But I shall die in peace, for she has given me peace."

"What are you saying?"

"If you knew how beautiful she was when she let me kiss her ... It was the first time I ever kissed a woman. But Christine, when I kissed her ... she didn't run. She was my beautiful wife and she didn't run!"

"Where is she?" demanded the Persian. "Where is Raoul? Are they dead? Have you killed them?"

■laugh away 一笑に付す　■write down 書き留める　■sink into 〜に沈む
■murderer 名人殺し　■die of 〜が原因で死ぬ　■run 動大急ぎで逃げる

ペルシャ人はこの話を残らず警察に伝えたが、笑いとばされてしまった。誰もが、彼は頭がおかしいのだと思った。他に方法もないので、ペルシャ人は知っていることをすべて書き留めることにした。何日も書き続け、ほぼ終わりかけた頃、家に客が訪れた。ひどくやせて背の高い、黒マントに仮面姿の男を、ダリウスが支えながらペルシャ人の部屋へ連れてきた。エリックだった！

　エリックはかなり弱っているようで、歩くのにダリウスの助けが必要だった。椅子に座りこむと、静かに言った。「やあ、古き友よ」

　「この人殺しめ！」ペルシャ人は怒鳴った。「フィリップ・ド・シャニーを殺したな！　それで、ラウルとクリスティーヌには何をした？」

　エリックは胸に手を当てて言った。「2人は今一緒にいる。そして自由だよ」

　「なんだって？」

　「私は死にかけていると、君に伝えに来た。クリスティーヌが恋しくて死にそうなのだ！　だが、平安のうちに死ねるだろう。クリスティーヌが平安をくれたから」

　「いったい何を言ってるんだ？」

　「見せてあげたかったよ、私にキスをさせてくれた時、彼女がどれほど美しかったか……。女にキスをしたのは生まれて初めてだった。だがクリスティーヌは、私がキスをした時……逃げなかったのだ。私の美しい妻は、逃げなかったのだよ！」

　「クリスティーヌはどこだ？」ペルシャ人は問い詰めた。「そしてラウルはどこだ？　2人は死んだのか？　おまえが殺したのか？」

"No, not dead … but free. How she begged for that young man's life! When the water was rising, she looked at me with her beautiful blue eyes. She said she would be my true, *living wife* if I saved you both. She said she would not kill herself. She would spend the rest of her life with me! And she meant it!"

Erik paused for a moment.

"I turned the scorpion and the water went back down. I carried you both out of there. We took care of you both until you were healthy again. That young man progressed quickly, but you, my friend, you are older and weaker. I did not know if you would make it. But you did, and when she saw that you would both live, she looked at me with such thanks in her eyes! Then … "

Erik had to stop again, for his emotions were making him weak.

"Then … I came near her as she looked at me with those blue eyes. She let me get closer and closer … and … *she let me kiss her!* Without closing her eyes or turning away, she let me kiss her on the forehead! My own mother wouldn't let me near her—she would run away and throw me my mask! Oh, how good it is to kiss someone you love! What happiness!

■mean 動 本気で〜と言っている ■pause 動 言葉を切る ■progress 動 向上する
■make it 回復する ■forehead 名 額

「いや、死んではいない……だが自由だ。あの若者の命を助けてほしいと頼んだ時の、クリスティーヌの必死さといったら！　水が上がってきた時、彼女はあの美しい青い瞳で私を見つめた。そして、もし２人を助けてくれたら、本物の生きた妻になると言った。自殺などしない。残りの人生をともに過ごすと言ったのだ！　彼女は本気だった！」

エリックはしばらく言葉を切った。

「私はサソリを回して、水を引かせた。そして君たちを運び出した。クリスティーヌと２人で、君たちが回復するまで看病した。あの若者はすぐに元気になったが、君はね、友よ、年を取っていたし弱っていた。助かるかどうかわからないと思ったよ。だが君は命を取り留めた。彼女は２人とも助かったのを見て、深い感謝の目で私を見たのだよ！　それから……」

エリックはまた休まねばならなかった。感情が高ぶったせいで、さらに弱ったからだ。

「それから……私が近づくと、彼女はあの青い瞳で私を見つめた。さらに近づいても彼女は動かなかった……そして……私にキスをさせてくれたのだ！　目を閉じることも、顔を背けることもなく、額にキスをさせてくれた！　母さえ私を近づけようとしなかったのに——母はいつも逃げ出して、私に仮面を投げつけたものだ！　ああ、愛する人にキスするというのは、なんと素晴らしいことか！　なんという幸福だろう！

I was so moved by it that I fell to my knees and began to cry. And do you know what she did? *She took my hand and cried with me!* Her tears fell on my face. They mixed with my own tears. We cried together! I knew it was the greatest happiness I would ever feel in my life … "

Erik was crying now and it was several minutes before he could continue. When he spoke again, it was very quietly.

"I looked at the gold ring on her finger—the ring I had given her. I took it off of her finger and put it into her hand. 'Take it!' I said. 'This is my wedding gift to you … to you and to *him*.' She looked at me with those blue eyes and asked what I meant. 'I know you love him. You can have a real life with him. I want to let you go, for you took pity on me and you cried for me!'"

Erik turned away at the memory of that moment.

"I went to Raoul where he was tied up. I untied him. She ran to him and they kissed. But Christine turned to me … she said thank you, and then *she kissed me!* I asked her to come back when I was dead. I wanted her to bury me with the gold ring under the opera. I asked her to wear the ring until that moment. She agreed. And that was the last time I saw her. But I am dying now, and if she keeps her promise, she will come back to me soon!"

■move 動 ～を感動させる ■take something off（物）を外す ■take pity on ～を哀れむ ■keep one's promise 約束を守る

あまりに感動した私は崩れ折れ、ひざをついて泣きだした。すると彼女はどうしたと思う？　なんと私の手を取って、一緒に泣いてくれたのだ！　彼女の涙が頬に落ちてきて、私の涙とひとつになった。私たちはともに泣いた！　人生であれほど幸福だったことはないよ……」

　今ではエリックは泣いていて、数分の間、話を続けられなかった。やっと話しだした時には、とても静かな声になっていた。
「私は彼女の指にはめた金の指輪を見た——私があげたものだ。それを指から抜いて、彼女の手の中に入れた。『持っていておくれ！』と私は言った。『これは結婚祝いだ……君とラウルへの』。彼女はあの青い瞳で私を見つめ、どういう意味か尋ねた。『彼を愛していることはわかっているよ。2人で本当の人生を送るがいい。行かせたいのだ。君が私を哀れみ、私のために泣いてくれたから！』」

　エリックはそのときのことを思い出し、顔を背けた。
「私はラウルを縛っているところへ近寄り、縄を解いた。彼女はラウルに走り寄ってキスをした。だがこちらを振り返り……ありがとうと言って、私にキスをしたのだ！　私は彼女に、私が死んだら帰ってきてほしいと言った。金の指輪とともにオペラ座の地下に埋めてもらいたいと。そして、そのときまでは指輪をしていてほしいと頼んだ。彼女は承知してくれた。それが、クリスティーヌを見た最後だ。でも今、私は死にかけている。彼女が約束を守ってくれるなら、もうすぐ私のもとへ帰ってくるだろう！」

The Persian asked no questions. He believed Erik, who sat in his room crying, remembering the most important moment of his life.

Soon, Erik rose to go. He gave the Persian a package that held all of Christine Daae's letters and a few of her belongings. He told the Persian that he believed the young couple had gone back to Christine's home town in Sweden. He also asked the Persian to let the couple know of his death by writing a simple message in the *Epoque*, the newspaper. Then, Erik left.

That was the last time the Persian saw Erik—the unhappy man who had been the Angel of Music and the opera ghost. Three weeks later, the *Epoque* ran this single line in the personal section:

"Erik is dead."

THE END

■package 名箱 ■belonging 名所有物 ■Epoque 名エポック《仏語、英語でtimeにあたる語》 ■run 動掲載する ■personal section 個人広告

ペルシャ人はもう何も聞かなかった。彼はエリックの話を信じた。エリックは彼の部屋に座ったまま涙を流し、人生でもっとも大切な瞬間を思い出していた。

　やがて、エリックは帰ろうと立ち上がった。彼はペルシャ人に、クリスティーヌ・ダーエの手紙全部と持ち物が入った箱を渡した。そして、若い恋人たちはきっと、スウェーデンにあるクリスティーヌの故郷の町へ帰ったのだろうと言った。また、自分が死んだら、『エポック』という新聞に簡単な伝言を書いて、２人に知らせてほしいとも頼んだ。そして、エリックは去った。

　ペルシャ人が、エリック——音楽の天使であり、オペラ座の怪人だった不幸な男——を見たのはこれが最後だった。３週間後、『エポック』紙の個人広告の欄に、この１行が載った。

「エリック死す」

終

● E-CATとは…
英語が話せるようになるための
テストです。インターネット
ベースで、30分であなたの発
話力をチェックします。

www.ecatexam.com

● iTEP®とは…
世界各国の企業、政府機関、アメリカの大学
300校以上が、英語能力判定テストとして採用。
オンラインによる90分のテストで文法、リー
ディング、リスニング、ライティング、スピー
キングの5技能をスコア化。iTEP®は、留学、就
職、海外赴任などに必要な、世界に通用する英
語力を総合的に評価する画期的なテストです。

www.itepexamjapan.com

[IBC対訳ライブラリー]
英語で読むオペラ座の怪人

2016年4月5日　第1刷発行
2021年1月24日　第2刷発行

原著者　　ガストン・ルルー

発行者　　浦　晋亮

発行所　　IBCパブリッシング株式会社
　　　　　〒162-0804 東京都新宿区中里町29番3号 菱秀神楽坂ビル9F
　　　　　Tel. 03-3513-4511　Fax. 03-3513-4512
　　　　　www.ibcpub.co.jp

印刷所　　株式会社シナノパブリッシングプレス
CDプレス　株式会社ケーエヌコーポレーションジャパン

© IBC Publishing, Inc. 2016

Printed in Japan

落丁本・乱丁本は、小社宛にお送りください。送料小社負担にてお取り替えいたします。
本書の無断複写（コピー）は著作権法上での例外を除き禁じられています。

ISBN978-4-7946-0405-7